The Lost Letters

Jeremy Void

Other books by Jeremy Void

Derelict America
(short stories and essays)

Nefarious Endeavors
(short stories and some poetry)

Smash a Lightbulb:
Poetry for Lowlifes
(poetry, prose, creative essays, and more)

Erase Your Face:
The SkullFuck Collection
(visual poetry)

Just a Kid
(experimental prose and poetry)

Sex Drugs & Violence:
Incomplete Stories for the Incomplete Human
(incomplete stories)

An Art Form:
The Crass Poetry Collection
(poetry)

My Story:
The Short Version
(my own drunkalogue)

I Need Help:
The SkullFuck Collection
(visual poetry)

THE LOST LETTERS

Poetry for Punks
like it was meant to be

Jeremy Void is back,
bringing to you that chaotic blend of prose and poetry he is known for.

Prose that run circles around you
Poems that make you think.

While most of America wastes their time watching television, getting fat on fast food

Jeremy Void

The Lost Letters

Copyright © 2015 by Jeremy Void

All Rights Reserved

No part of this book may be reproduced, scanned, or distributed in any print or electronic form without permission. Please do not participate in or encourage piracy of copyrighted materials in violation of the author's rights. Purchase only authorized editions.

ISBN Number:
978-0-578-17178-4

ChaosWriting Press

It's A Mindfuck

www.chaoswriting.net

To Tiana Butts

Contents

The Serenade —— 1
An American Controversy —— 3
Under the Pavilion —— 6
wanna be a God —— 8
Before My Eyes —— 11
A Devout Punk Rocker —— 14
Lost in a Rut —— 17
Forcing the Crap —— 19
Letters to Lost Friends —— 22
It's Not That Easy —— 30
No Hope —— 31
Another Poem Called "Fuck You" —— 32
A Walk Through the Jungle —— 35
My Arch Nemesis —— 39
Something to Feel —— 40
maybe something —— 43
A Curious Love Affair —— 46
Too Much to Think —— 48
Late in the Night —— 51
My Insanity —— 52
A Downward Spiral —— 53
War at Home —— 57
Any Moron —— 58
The Lost Letter —— 61
Sleepless Beauty —— 63

Dance to the Apocalypse —— 65
A Hopeless Struggle —— 67
To Be Seen by You —— 69
Come with Me —— 70
Futility —— 71
Open-Mike at Spring Lake Ranch —— 74
Not Enough —— 79
An Unstoppable Force —— 81
It's no fun/// —— 82
Join the Lost —— 85
A Punk Rock Song —— 87
An Imperfect Circle —— 89
The Lost —— 94
So Alone —— 96
An Outburst at the Beach —— 100
inertia (n) —— 105
At the Top of the World —— 108
No Comment —— 110
Censor Censorship —— 111
Barely Alive —— 113
The Light Will Do That to You —— 115
My Cocaine Cherry —— 118
What You Need to Know —— 122
A Pit of Despair —— 123
Pledge Allegiance to ... what? —— 126
Redemption —— 127
Suffering —— 131

The Streets aren't safe —— **132**
A World of Our Own —— **135**
A RANT, so to speak —— **136**
A Dreamer, a Schemer, and a Freak —— **141**
Your Problem Is Your Problem —— **143**
Sinfulness Is Godliness —— **145**
In Search of the Truth —— **146**
Lost in a Sequence of Screams —— **148**
On Picking Sides —— **156**
Words That Heal —— **158**
Little Derelict —— **160**
Bruised & Bloodied —— **162**
A Plan for Greatness —— **164**
The Holy Ghost —— **167**
A Song of Dreams —— **169**
The Next Big Punk Rock Hit —— **173**
Junky Pride —— **175**
I Am a Fish —— **177**
For the Painter —— **178**
Into the Madness —— **179**
For Medicinal Purposes —— **181**
Not Good Enough —— **183**
My Psychedelic Suicide —— **184**
To Be a Household Name —— **204**

The Serenade

"This one time I wrote a poem for a girl, read it to her, but then I told her it wasn't for her."

— Jeremy Void

I thought I heard something that made me high
it made me hot
You see I'm a nervous kid only I'm 28,
stripped of pills that made me calm.
Stripped of drugs which made me cool.
Stripped of life as I kissed the moon.

I lived fast and slow, cold and hot
I just don't know.
I can't get these words to flow when
I talk, but I **know** The Words and I can **use** The Words
to blow you away.

I'll make you high
I'll make you hot
Come with me and we'll
rob the lot.
Let's dance together beneath the moon
rip off our skin and get real crude.

I don't speak of sex
I don't speak of appeal

Jeremy Void

I don't speak of recklessness
I speak of real.

I speak of you and I on the kill
I speak of you and I getting thrills
I speak of you and I running around aimlessly
I speak of the sky melting as the stars shine bright and sick.

What do you say? A single night
you and I in the raw.
A single night of chills and we'll be biting
and scratching as roosters squeal.

I don't speak of sex
I don't speak of appeal
I don't speak of being
just another lover
cuz I just want your number and
we can go from there....

All I speak of is
you and I and one night
you'll simply never forget.

An American Controversy

I can't draw but I've
got something better for you
much much better, a
moving picture told with
words

here I go....

There's a woman
holding a shopping bag
who is getting raped
by Uncle Sam—

on TV

In the living room is
a fat man stuffing his face
with KFC——yum yum yum.
His erection grows as Uncle
Sam thrusts into the woman.

Good old-fashioned tele
vision. Good old-fashioned
redneck eating commercialized crap

Jeremy Void

and getting a hard-on watching
this woman take it up the ass.

Only Uncle Sam dawns a Hitler mustache,
and he has a menacing grin
spreading from ear to ear

and the woman is smiling....

Why is she smiling?
Cuz she's too dim to realize
the reality of it.... She doesn't realize
that this is what America is doing
to her.... buy buy buy
spend spend spend

Money is good and right
and magazines are god-sent
from the heavens above.
She consumes it while dabbing makeup
on her face to hide the grotesqueness
that she sees when she wakes up every
morning.

Every single morning....

and beside her, her husband is just as
fat and gross, only
he's got a high-paying job
that can afford her senseless buying.
Thank god for that.
So she puts up with his own atrocities

just for access to a limitless credit card.

An American Controversy

Back up, maybe her husband
is the fat redneck watching his wife
on TV getting raped by Uncle Sam.

He'd be eating it up///

Under the Pavilion

The fire burns in the grill,
the flames reaching through the steel girder
like a caged animal trying to break out.
People stand or sit, scattered in and
out of the pavilion, senseless chatter, mind-numbingly dull,
drifts through the airwaves. The smell of cooking
charcoal breaches my nostrils, a dull, chocky smell
that is kind of soothing out here in the middle of
the woods—it smells like camping. Which
is to be expected; it makes perfect sense.

A group of three or four stand talking a couple
feet from the fiery grill; I look over to describe
their poses but instead notice how the fire
has died. Oh shit, I think. That sucks!
"The fire," I say to the guy manning the grill.
"The fire has— Oh." Sense creeps into my
clueless head when I catch the thin wisps
of steam trailing up from the charcoal, realizing
that that's the point, the fire goes and the charcoal
stays hot—hot enough to cook the food at least.

I'm hungry; all this talking about
food has worked up my appetite.
Last night I spent the duration in Ben's

Under the Pavilion

pickup truck just reading til the sun came up
and alcoholics emerged from every orifice
in Emerald Lake State Park.
Yesterday the only thing I'd eaten
was two cheeseburgers and a
medium fries from McDoncld's; we
stopped at the drive-through on our way
here.

All night long my stomach growled like
an angry beast's mating call, deep and rough and scary.
I usually have trouble focusing when
I'm hungry like that, but fortunately I brought
a book with a rather decent beginning that I
found myself relating to—a book that literally
just came in the mail yesterday afternoon.
Talk about perfect timing.

The food is being prepared; more
people have come down here to
conjure, more voices joining the cacophony of
mindlessness. I guess that's the point of
small talk, although I myself find it rather
difficult to converse and relate on a
superficial level. What should
I say? When should I say it?
My own racing thoughts the only hindrance
I can think of, the only force keeping
me from conversing with my fellow, friendly
alcoholics.

wanna be a God

i dont wanna be loved....
i wanna be cherished.
i dont wanna be hated....
i wanna be banished.

i dont want you to see me
as a useless human being.
as a man who wont accomplish nothing,
but as a ruler a king a god who will
break you down & kick you around
& fuck you till the cows
all die...

i dont wanna be this
i wanna be that
i wanna be better
badder
a kid on the skid who grew up
to kick   your fuckin ass.

all i want is that
i want more
i dont wanna be your whore
but a guy whos raw to the core
a lord a deity a guy who will bring you up

wanna be a God

& throw you down & twist you up
& kick you fuck you eat you
see you here & there & everyfuckinwhere.

i dont wanna be lost
i dont wanna be found.
i dont wanna be up
i dont wanna be down.

i dont want you around.
but i need you now now now///
i want you here so i can tear you apart....

i want to be YOUR ruler
not your loser
but the overseer crueler
& ruder & vicious a king
of the losers.

i want to live fast as you
kiss my fucking ass.
i dont wanna look back
i wanna move forward
& crazy & cruel as i bark orders
at you & you
OBEY me—thats all i want

to be a god a king a mean motherfucker
who will spit on you & shit on you
& put you down in all the worst ways.

thats what im saying

im angry & pent up
im twisted & demented

Jeremy Void

lost & losing & lost
& i wanna be cruising
all over you....

Before My Eyes

I sit on a ledge
staring out yonder, watching
as the pigs are fed
the birds have fled
and I wonder briefly
what it means
to be dead.

Life is like a puppet
we use it till it breaks.
Like a computer
pressing buttons till
it quakes.

I sit here on an island
watching as the boats
slue through and about.
I watch them stammer over
waves and steady when the rolling
deadens.

What's the meaning of life?
I find myself asking when the wakes
even out to a minute shifting.
My pondering strengthens and then

Jeremy Void

the rush of water heightens to an epic surge
that pulls my focus away from the prior
ruminations that only serve to make me mad.

I'm frequently finding myself bored
lost
angry   and wasteful
wasted
washed up on the beach that lies
in the middle of denial.

My life is crumbling
to a million and one pieces.
I tried AA meetings to
piece it back together,
but the attempt has backfired

and now I'm sober
with no place to go.

No options left
in this fragment of a dream.
I sit here and try
trying my hardest
just to fall asleep.

The bats flutter and dive.
They rise and flicker in the night.
I watch them in dark flashes
free to be fast and wild.
I wonder what it would be like
to have that kind of power
to be that kind of liberated.
but only in a dream will it ever come to be

Before My Eyes

only I just can't fall asleep

so I sit here and I watch....

A Devout Punk Rocker

There was a day when I was
a devout Punk rocker—THE
        Punk rocker.

I believed in listening to bad
music, having a bad time, and doing bad.

I believed in beating my head against the wall
until my skull cracks.
        Never seen any other of my friends
          attempt such a fete.

It started with the name GG Rotten.
As crazy as GG Allin
and as rotten as Johnny Rotten/// Coined by

older Punks who were intrigued by my
pissing in the gas tank of the parked car.

I lived the fastest, the loudest, and I hadn't seen
anybody live up to my standards.

All I see today are kids who know
nothing about what a bad time means.
Kids who if you told them Punk rock sucked

A Devout Punk Rocker

they'd defend it saying I'm an asshole.
Well it does suck—as in bad music.
    If it was good,
        I wouldn't listen to it
            this is true….

Punk was never meant to be "good,"
as in the name "Punk."
It's not an accident that the word used to label
these kids was as bad as "cunt" in the time
they adopted the name.

Kids don't know that.
They think, Oh it's got a catchy melody
a fast beat that matches my ADD
and lyrics about rebellion,
    and I hate my school
        like any other of my peers,
            so where do I sign up?

No you're missing the point.
Signing up defeats the purpose.
That's what I don't get, it's not some
flavor of the month you can be a part of
when convenient and leave
when you're at the risk of getting your
head kicked in by jocks.

It's a stance *against* what's
popular, and if Punk rock
    as if it hasn't already
became popular, I'd duck out of the scene
    as if I haven't already

There was a day when I was

Jeremy Void

a devout Punk rocker—THE
        Punk rocker,
        but not anymore cuz
        the scene has gotten rather lame
        over the years....

<u>Besides, it's just not the same anymore.</u>

Lost in a Rut

I write, I do art.
I wait and I pace.
Anxiety can be a bitch
when you have nobody
to direct it at....

I wonder
pray to the sky
why nobody cares about
little old me, and the things
that I do.

I'm a terminal
social suicide, making new friends
and losing them constantly.
I'm destined to be no one
destined to nothing
nowhere and it's no fun.

Why me is my anthem.
I thought one day I'd
get over this feeling, the feeling of
hopelessness.

THE FEELING THAT

Jeremy Void

every attempt is futile
and therefore why should I care.

I don't know.
You tell me.
Help me see the light.
Help me get through this
emptiness I'm losing myself to.

I'm lost in a rut   a rut, and
it sucks. I want out now.
Let me out of this world.
Take me on your space shuttle
next time you're in town.
Fly me around the moon so that
for once I can feel good and alive
and for once I wont haveta cry.

AND I CRY....

Well, not really; I don't exactly know how.

Forcing the Crap
(or) Letting It Flow

Stop trying, it
'll come on its own.
Stop forcing or
you'll lose your mind on this
poem that's supposed to
shine light on ... something or
another.

Your mind is a fragile tool
and if you push too hard
it'll snap
in half
leaving you with a series of
flaccid thoughts; blackened ideas
that wrap around you like
cement.

I keep guessing what
comes next
in this life
how it will end and I
can go on to
the next one.

Jeremy Void

I keep dreaming about a different
reality, one with lots and lots of
freedom, dwelling in a fabricated
world where nothing is ordinary
and everything is
simply
<u>out to lunch</u>
      like me.

But my mind races fiercely and
it keeps me hostage
to my thought process.
To think I thought I was
leading it, but I was
wrong again—

I'm used to being wrong.

This is the world I'm in
this is where I live
and I can easily say
I despise this life, but how
would I if I know no other
and have not a single reference point
to go on.

I sit back and observe
analyze the ways of others
watching what makes them whole
what causes them to snap
and I sit back and wait for
something bad to happen
to them

because then

Forcing the Crap

and only then
will I feel good about myself.

I know it's pathetic and
I'm sorry to break it to you
so honestly like that
but would you have preferred I
flung a stinking clump of shit
in your face.

Letters to Lost Friends

Friends come and go
in life, some good and
some bad, and some of your
friends vanish as though
into thin air. AND what would
I say to them if I could
       try and
       reel them
          in /// for only a minute.

1.
Bergie my old pal
who I'd known since
I was a wee little one
who had resentments against
me cuz I was into Punk.
This metal head converted though
in the later years of his life and then,
now having seen life my way,
through my eyes,
decided to give me a try—
a go as a friend.

Bergie the beat boxer who

Letters to Lost Friends

used to crash at my pad regularly
because of troubles at home
and we'd stay up all night and shoot
the shit—humorously of course
as he was always up for
a sick, perverted joke—
        that's Bergie in a nut shell.

He told me the weekend I came
and visited him in college was
the craziest weekend he'd had all year
maybe of his whole time attending
Westfield State.

We had good times, Bergie and I, sitting
on my stoop and spitting and cursing
as we laughed and talked and talked and
laughed, while he and Kristen turned
everything I said into a song—like
"Sitting and Spitting and Shitting on
the Stoop Is Fun," to name a few.

Our riotous times creeping through
Newton Center staying up all night and watching
the trains go by. Were you there when
we spotted the ghost train?

Big fucking Bergie, we had our turmoil
as well, as all my friends had gone through it
I know, but our friendship would always mend
over and we'd go on goofing off like the fuckup Punk
rockers we were born to be.

Like, when you agreed to record Lethal Erection
and I had promised you the band would not drink

Jeremy Void

since this was your college we're talking about
and I, me and me only, showed up blitzed
out of my mind
and snuck off between songs to take a hit
of the flask filled with Jack Daniels I had
stowed away in my inner pocket.

For my rampage of madness I wrecked around your college
that night
I know you were pissed and it took quite a bit of time
to mend that
but our bond was stronger than a little
drunken mishap like this.

Oh Bergie, you fell in love
with a girl who you thought was perfect
a girl you'd known for
the longest time you had told me
and you married her and went off to
North Dakota to live the happy,
married life, which isn't as happy
as you had thought you'd come
to find out later on.

Last time we spoke you were scolding me
for insulting a friend of yours, but not a friend
of mine, via Facebook. You said, rather bluntly,
as was your style, Next time you get drunk
lock your doors, shut off your phone, and
turn off your goddamn Internet, YOU FUCK!
and with that I plopped on my butt, folded up
my knees inside my arms, and bowed my head
and began crying.
At the time I was walking to an AA meeting.

Letters to Lost Friends

Bergie, man, I miss you, and
I'm sure you don't miss my mayhem,
as nobody does—well, except Chuck
but he's a major fucking exception—
but this is me and this is you and we
were brothers, our bond strong as diamonds
able to withstand a tremendous hurricane
of turmoil.

Maybe you're sick of it
fed up with my shit
having lost hope for this
lost cause, but I'd give anything
just to say to you
that I've fucking changed so fucking much.

2.
What the fuck Chuck!
What the-what the-what the fuck Chuck!
From the moment you picked me up
at the Haverhill train station after
having nearly mowed me down in your truck
you motherfucker
I had a feeling we'd stick together.
We'd been through a lot, you and I
from sucking down the crack pipe
to shoving spikes in our veins
from huddling together in an alleyway somewhere
cold and miserable and hungover with a major
fiending for more of the last drug
we had taken.

You and I it was chaos.

Jeremy Void

How many times had we been
arrested together?
How many court hearings
did we share?
I'd like to say I had learned
a lot from you, but I can't
think of what, although I know
you had learned a lot from me,
none of it good and I'm sad to stay
I created a monster.

You were my best bud.
We drove up to the Cape together
and laughed riotously the entire
ride with jokes about blowing lines
off the traffic cop's badge, and about our
adventures in fancy dining—I mean it
it was a riot, you and I.

I remember you would take off in a charge
while walking from Harvard Square to
Central Square and jump in front of an old
lady, a young man, a girl, a boy,
and start dancing, as though dancing with them
except your dance partner's a little creeped-out
by you.

We sat on the train and got barked at
by the driver who was fed up with
the loud Punk rock roaring from
my boom box.
You danced on the roof of a Jaguar while
I kicked out the mirrors.

I remember after the first show Lethal Erection

Letters to Lost Friends

played with you as our guitarist, after the set,
you grabbed someone else's guitar off the wall
and brought it down on the floor—smash crash, shatter.
You and I we stuck together like glue
and we huffed it too.

But now you're gone, you just
will not grow up. You have five kids.
Six, by now? And you're still a
little kid yourself. And from what
I've heard you've become a cunt too,
which is not something I had taught you.
Respect and loyalty towards friends was
key and when you and I hung out frequently
you would have agreed.

But I realize now you were less of a friend
and more of a lacky
and in my absence you had to find someone else
to latch onto, a boy named Craig who I liked then
but dislike now because of the way you two had
been ganging up on Mike who at that point
in time really needed you as a friend

Not something I had taught you.

3.
Andy
Fat Andy, who used to
bully me, leaving a ladder of scars
all the way up both my shins
with his steel toed boots.
We were friends though, and

Jeremy Void

I was the sucker, but you were
the liar, spinning fabricated stories
of glory, going to prison and thriving,
for one, or about your career
as an undefeated cage fighter.
You said I'm the only guy who had
kicked your ass, you realize that.
Me, skinny Jeremy St. Chaos
strung out on crack and everything else
he put into his system.

But aside from all that we were friends
and you fucked my first girlfriend after
we had broken up
        that's fucking gross
           my own dick took years to recover
           from that dirty hag's hole.

But I did get revenge on you when
that one girl, Sara I think her name was,
sucked me off in the bathroom while
you sat in the living room nearly passed out.
Then we went out back and I turned your face
into mashed potatoes, and you turned my fist
into a used tampon.

This was our friendship, I look back at how silly
at how foolish we were, but in the end I made
you the fool when you took my
cock in your mouth
        ——you sick fuck
        I don't even know
        where that's been.

Were we competing for something?

Letters to Lost Friends

Maybe you were jealous of my awesomeness
my playing in a band and playing the star.
You sat through this and watched my destruction
and pretended that you had my back by
telling my parents about my crack days.

But on the other hand, you did save my life.
When I downed a bottle of pills, you were
the one to gut punch me and shove your fingers
down my throat—with little success though, but
you did call 911.

We'd been through a lot, you and I
seen a side of life most people will
never lay their eyes upon.

We had our problems but we had our
fun and through it all our blood was the thickest
we stuck together no matter fucking what
always forgiven, always mended, and we ripped
up the city like the badasses we were.

———

To be continued....

It's Not That Easy

There are things I've gotta do
    so many things,
and yet I don't do them.   Why?

Why can't I just do the things
I know I've gotta do?
Make the calls, put in the time.

It really is just that simple.

BUT I CAN'T
        BUT I CAN'T
                BUT I fucking CAN'T!!!

It might be simple
    and trust me it is,
but it isn't that easy
        not in the least bit....

Pressure's building up.
Fate's racking my brain.
I know what I've gotta do
what I've gotta do to end this
    pain.

                But no, nothing
                ever gets done.

No Hope

I think there are small fragments of hope
manifesting in the most obscurest of ways
They come
and they go, and this hope you speak of
is a dream we seek
and we seek it, but it never
materializes, so we're
lost
walking down death's road
the reaper waiting at the end
a gleaming, bleak smile wrapped around
his bony, albino face.
The human race is doomed
and the devil sits up on his thrown
watching his masterpiece grow
and fester and
kill us all.
But me, I try to stand tall
amid all the waste
the wasted life forms lurking
and I try to stay true
amid the destruction
which would otherwise destroy me.

Another Poem Called "Fuck You"

"Thinking aloud may hurt, I'm on the alert."
— "Titanic Reaction" by 999

I try to stay true to myself
I try to be me at all times
and if you don't like it
if you find it offensive or brash
if you think I'm mean and crass
if you think my writing is just disturbing trash
well, I'm sorry but but but

I've gotta admit this
confess that I'm not writing to
please you or anyone
I'm not writing to satisfy your desire
for happy-go-luck crap, for empty
poems about butterflies spanning
their wings and flapping through the
green and beautiful garden that glows
like heaven and shines like diamonds
in the sun.

I say it how I see it, and if you don't
like my twisted, fucked-up perspectives
on the world, my perverse sense of humor
if you don't like it

Another Poem Called "Fuck You"

all I've gotta say is

FUCK YOU

I'm not writing to please you
it's not my responsibility to see to
your own happiness which is fake anyway—
we all know the truth about that.

So
FUCK YOU
if you think I'm a dick.
FUCK YOU if when
you read my writing you perceive
me as nothing but a prick.

Well, guess what,
I am.

But I'm not writing to satisfy your need
for a fabricated world with phony smiles
and phony lives that are desperate for
happy, empty distractions.

It's not my job to make you happy.
If I made you happy, I wouldn't be
doing my best as a controversial,
provocative poet whose hope is to
offer you a mirror into your own
sick sickness.

That's right, you're sick.

So FUCK YOU
if you think I'm a dick.

Jeremy Void

FUCK YOU if when
you read my writing you perceive
me as nothing but a prick.

Cuz I am and the fact that
you don't like it doesn't change
a goddam thing.

A Walk Through the Jungle

I walked through the jungle this afternoon
saw kids on bikes pedaling up the road, cars
buzzing past me, junkies and crack heads huddled
in an alleyway somewhere.

The wind bristled off my skin
warm and refreshing the way it brushed
past me and the sun shone from above
like from a light tower to guide me through
the jungle....

Buildings were painted, graffiti art crossing the walls
in bubbly arrays of paint that looked randomly
depicted but ordered just enough to convey
a message to me
and said messages were conveyed, but in some
the messages were lost and it made me sad.

I passed the coffee shop on my right
customers bustling in and out the door
it was fairly crowded for a Sunday in Rutland
coffees served and drunk as happy-go-lucky
customers sat and conversed in chairs, around
tables, and I stood outside the window
looking in at them until

Jeremy Void

a pretty young girl caught my eyes and sneered
straight at me...

Afraid she might complain to her big, tough-looking
boy toy that some strange older guy
was peeping in and he looked crazy and queer
I continued down the road.

Down this way the jungle gets darker
the world gets harder
and the sky gets farther and I proceeded
on my way as the sun dropped and everything
unfolded around me like I was lost
in a kaleidoscope. I wandered and
the world dropped out from beneath me.
I plunged into a world less travelled where animals
loped along showing off their scarred and tattooed
skin, their googly eyes laced with sinister sneers.

I kept an alert eye watching as the world melted away
as pipes crashed into bricks, clashing with skin
as chains jangled and rang, jittery and harsh.
The darkness bright with mischief, I crept into
the madness like a lost pup.
I was weary of the animals that came stampeding
through the alleys, the stark stench like burning rubber
the harsh sounds like household items thrashing
crashing
nasty and brash
stammering down the stairs.

A big, black gorilla emerged from the alley before me.
He held up some wooden club of sorts
with symbols galore etched into the wood.
He looked mean

A Walk Through the Jungle

and mad, pointed the menacing club my way
and before he could holler
which he did—eventually
I took off running, with a cacophony of feet
cluttering against the sidewalk behind me.
I clipped left and the banging of Timberland boots
against concrete ebbed for only a second but then
picked up harder and louder and I looked back
and saw that the stampede had gained momentum.
I hurried as they gained speed and got closer to me
and closer
and closer
closer
closer.

<u>I was cut off then.</u>
<u>They stopped me there.</u>
<u>I was surrounded.</u>
<u>They all had fierce stares.</u>
<u>I looked left and right for an</u>
<u>escape route but it never came.</u>

I was surrounded by a
pack of apes closing in on
me and they were holding clubs
and chains
and knifes
and looked mean and hard
and scary, and then
they charged.

I was caught up in the volley
of fists and feet
dropping into me.
I held up my hands in front of

Jeremy Void

my face, but there were too many of them
and the blows kept coming
plunging
slamming through the shield I held up

fuck me....

My Arch Nemesis

The thing I hate most about you
is
the fact
that I see me when I look into
your filthy fucking eyes.

Something to Feel

Only one thing I cared about, only one thing I wanted—it wasn't money or love or sex or money or anything like that. No it was nothing superficial, it was a dream—which had wrapped me up in its electric tendrils as I struggled to breathe. I wanted to FEEL, that's all I wanted, all I needed in this world—was emotions that could lift me up and kick me down, make me scream uncle out loud.

FEELINGS was something I lacked back then. I used substances to replace the numbness, the terminal jaded feeling that wound me up in a blank cocoon, another member of the blank youth, a blank soul that drifted through the blank harvesting fields to pillage the blank plantations—but there was none, it was so utterly blank and without it I was lost. I was jaded lost and hungry for affection, but for me affection meant connecting and connecting meant coexisting and coexisting meant CHANGE, which is not something I was willing to do, couldn't commit to it, not in the least, because I was me and only me and I wanted to be nobody else—but me. Except a version of ME that had FEELINGS.

I prescribed myself a back alley lobotomy what with all the drugs and booze I consumed because I thought it looked cool on me, I thought it made me better and smarter and brought me closer to the things that I seeked—feelings, that is.

Something to Feel

EMOTIONS

I was not an emotional guy, I was selfish and stubborn and would do just about anything to get my way, I was a narcissist from the lowest level of life, I was the narcissist the common folk resisted and I felt like a king in my own mind but in the real world I was only a mere cretin, a kid who grew up in the wrong time with the wrong set of rules lurking over his head—and I fought them tooth and nail, I was tough, I got my ass kicked a lot but I always stood right back up and continued to fight back for my rights—see what good that all did? I was resilient, guess you could say. A tenacious cretin who always lost but felt proud of his failures and losses so it seemed like a win to me, like a victory, like I had kicked your fuckin ass in the end and ground it into the dirt, stamped my heel on your head as your teeth crumbled against the curb you had been biting—stupid you. But those small anti-victories, with lack for a better word, didn't get me any closer to FEELINGS—in fact it brought me the other way. Turned me into a stone-cold losing machine. The biggest fuckup you'd ever seen. A failure in all sense of the word, but hey I always had drugs I could rely on and they would never let me down————until they let me down and when they did I fell off the ground and into the sky flapping my nonexistent wings as I fell out of the Ozone layer and continued to flail as I plummeted into deep space—the story of my life.

Out in space there were no FEELINGS. No alien whose shoulder I could rest my head on and cry. Just a jaded sensation that wrapped me up in a bleak cocoon manifesting in the most blankest of futures, a blank outcome resulting from a blank past where I had got nothing done, I mean nothing—*nada*. That's how I lived my life for the longest time you see, only I felt like it was a more hands-on way to exist than that of the common folk who simply picked success off of trees and bought achievements at the Eminence Store. It's easy for the common folk to succeed, they

Jeremy Void

were born into triumph, into a world where only the odd folk—the folk just like me—would fail.

So I became jaded, with a general hatred for the common folk, the folk who won every single round, beat the system when it was beneficial to; and jaded I'll tell you is nowhere closer to MY goals. I was lost in outer space. Lost in a track of failings and shortcomings and I just couldn't get out. It ate at my soul until there was nothing left and that resilient side of me that I had mentioned earlier dwindled and dwindled and dwindled until there was nothing left of it either—and I was no longer a lost soul, but a crumbling, defeated soul who crept through the world with only one purpose in mind—which was to make the world pay for my misfortunes. If you knew me, I probably screwed you in my own numb fashion, a fashion lacking even the most simplest of feelings…..
You see, that's how I fell apart….

maybe something

I crave something
    a fix
        maybe something

I sit back and wait
    in my room
      the white walls
        getting brighter
        closing in
they breathe

I want (need) something
    to make me feel whole
      to lift me up
      and kick me down
I want of hit of
whatever the girl's smoking
burrow my head
between her legs
    sniff her panties
        maybe something

I want to live wild
fast and alive dashing
    through my mind

Jeremy Void

      on the epoch of
      the universe

I don't want to care
about anything
about what the spectators
think of me
      I know it's bad
      and I want to
      stop my head from racing
      my eyes blinking rapidly
      looking inward
and my brain is throbbing

I gotta stop thinking
that's my problem
      who even cares?
      I do and it's
      so useless I know but I just can't
          stoppit!

I count the sheep
try to sleep
the herd ebbs
      in my head
growing larger
      too many to count
      1 – 2 – 3——   it's
      no use and I just
      can't seem to fall asleep

I need a hit
a stab a tear
a poke maybe
      something

maybe something

it goes way over my head

bashing my head until
I simply drop
was   one of my favorite
pasttimes—it goes like this:
        cock / swing / smash
        the pain absorbs me
        my head swims with glee
        and for a moment
            your life is lost
            on me

like I wrote
   said
   cared
   wondered
   brooded
            a useless rumination
            like a crown of thorns
it's all so pointless
      maybe something
      maybe something
           if only she was here
           I held her in my arm

it's like they taught us   (in church / at school))))
      death is
           THE ultimate high!

A Curious Love Affair
with Alexandra Schaffer

Staring listlessly out the window

blissfully harmonizing my mind

The roof with the broken shingles is bathed in the pale blue morning light

The pitter-patter of rain dribbling on the roof sounds warm and delightful

I close my eyes and let the sound cover me

But when the darkness snaps into place I'm off in another world

And as my hand moves along my thigh, fingers nervously picking at the crusted gash that I don't remember getting...

my eyes surge open and where I awaken is some place all together

different, I focus on the bench in the park where we sat that day

the bench where one day way back when we fought and another day forgave and finally we lay there as the sun crested over the hills

Your head resting on my lap as we laughed at nothing at all

Your eyes glistened beneath the disentigrating sun as the dark sky unfolded and spread its sinister wings that embraced us.

A Curious Love Affair

I hated you because I loved you so much but my lips always found their home on yours and the night had a way of softening all the hard feelings

You were mine and mine only but when I got you here, I wanted you no more and kicked you away only to plead for your return to my arms.

But you were gone, lost to me like so many moments in time long dead and decayed in the back of my mind

So I stand in the sea as the waves overtake my soul.

Drowning in regret and feeling wrecked and lost

Because I know I've escaped the blundering spell you cast on me but when I see you again I'll be lost in your swirling blue eyes that hypnotize me, and it makes me mad

But still I want to be trapped by you, need to feel you, need to taste you, and that will never change, never

These hopeless yearnings, full of hope and my guts are churning, cause the world to break apart and the little shards to billow up past me and I wave goodbye.

As I look at the broken shingles which are now shrouded in early darkness, they don't look so broken, and I wonder did I make all of this up?

Too Much to Think

Life—glorious life
Death—haunted by life
Confusion—the two entities blend
together, and I don't know which
for which, it all seems so
mysterious to me.

I'm dying
     or
I'm living
     or
I'm contemplating why
WHY
WHY—why why why!
You can't live when you're trying
to master the secrets that life holds.
You will never know the secrets
that life holds. You might try
you might die
you might live your life, but not
while you're asking them why....

I'm stuck contemplating
Am I living
     or

Too Much to Think

am I dying
or do I just merely exist, floating
through the motions, like an empty vessel
rocking and riding the waves as they
take it for a ride.

I spend much of my time wondering
and wondering only serves as an
obstruction, an insidious obstruction
sent to divert your precious life on
a blind course through limbo.
I am not a robot, I do more than exist,
I do more than what my masters
have programmed me for.
I will kill, I will fight.
I will get my thrills any way necessary,
impeding on your dastardly impositions
that only cause my brain to ache

and it does ache.

So I say to you I'm
stuck in a familiar brood, a churning
of emotions that makes me
hate living and resent my mom
and my dad
and especially God
for putting me here. Bringing me
this.

THIS

What is this? If only I knew
I could get on with this life and leave
the brooding behind, but I don't know

Jeremy Void

I don't know
I don't know, and
it makes me sad to know
that I know nothing
and I just merely exist in someone else's
(someone else who's not me))))
        ——someone else's reality.

Late in the Night

It's late in the night, and I feel I feel I feel like I'm waiting for something.   But what>>>> It's late in the night and my mind races something fierce, speculating or whatever it is that my mind does late in the night. It's so late so late and the whole world sleeps. I think about things as the whole world sleeps. Sometimes I wonder about things, pondering deeply and spaciously until my pondering ceases and I fall asleep
It's late in the night and I hate I hate that there's nothing to do here. I sit up in my room and wonder why there's not a thing to do.   NOTHING at all////
The nighttime has a mind too, a big mind fat mind, a mind that makes me feel oh so fine and alone and sometimes I like it but sometimes I don't,,,,,,,,,,,,,,,,,,,,,,,,,,,,,

The mind races while the body sleeps, my mind's hollow and my body feels steep, like a hill rising through hell and dropping to the depths of heaven.   So Alone.

Sometimes I hope for zzzombies==   for an epic apocalypse, for something that would make life better   and more interesting too: something I could do in this hole other than just doing myself like I did just yesterday and tonight, again and again until my skin blisters and bruises and I fall asleep with my dick in my hand.

I'm utterly bored, fairly alive. and in an epic wasted monotonous slumbr~~~

My Insanity

When the world gets overtaken
by blackness
by darkness
most people will go running for the hills
but me
I'll embrace it
I'll lap it up
the madness
the sickening desolate plains
the world turning dayglo
everything undergoing insanity
it's all I could ask for in life.
I'd fit right in.
The world would be mine
and I'll laugh and frolic in the flames.

Insane, yeah I know it is,
but it's my insanity
and if you're gonna be insane
you might as well own it.

A Downward Spiral

I fought
I ran
I stole
I lied

The world was mine
it seemed, and I lived
I lived
I lived
for no one but myself///

I had no cause
I had no hope
it was hopeless, now that
I look back on it
and I'm
still to this day
shocked that I had
survived all the mayhem.

Broken glass
drugs
booze
fast women

Jeremy Void

The world spins
I was dizzy
lost in a downwardspin
I was spinning
couldn't hold on

falling
and I thought
the fall would never
end.

I couldn't hold on
any longer
death was right around
the corner
and I taunted the
grim reaper
taunted him and he never
came for me.

He never came for me.

The cops they tried
to stop me
tried to hold me down
but not jails
nor institutions could
stop my fall.

It was madness
It was blackness
oblivion you couldn't
imagine.

I stepped closer to the edge

A Downward Spiral

but it was stretching,
growing farther
and I was running toward it
running toward the drop
but my edge was running
from me.

Guns
knives
needles
trannies wanting to
kick my face in.

Crazy
the lights were out
sniffing glue
fucking
and throwing it all away.

The music played
I was in front
I held the mike
and I moved all night long
moved to the rhythm
moving in this Punk rock groove.

The lights were out
the colors faded to black
everything went blurry
fuzzy
liquidated, a splash of motion
a splash of motion
I was turning
turning
turning

Jeremy Void

and everywhere I looked
it was all the same.

Drugs
booze
girls
fun fun fun

and the fun would never
ever
end, but it did
and I was falling
fast
the glass slashing me
the water splashing

I was immersed
having fallen into
another puddle
another broken law.

I didn't know what I
would
do
about
this....

The only
solution
I could think of
was another hit
another sip
another shot
another line

and IF I COULD DO IT
every   thing   would   be   fine///

War at Home

THE WORLD IS BROKEN AND I FIX IT
with the blunt edge of a sledge hammer.

They say these guys are creeps
they say these gals are freaks.
They're hypocrites of the worst degree
they lie and steal and cheat.
They will do you in and not look back
they will cuss you out and it's not an act.

But what do I do??

MY LIFE IS SHATTERED AND FIX IT
with the crisp point of a pick axe.

Any Moron

Guy says to me, "Any moron
could write down a bunch of swears
and call it a poem."

This, because I said, "Any moron
could play a cover song."

He took it way out of proportion
and I tried to do the right thing
tried to apologize to him and mend it
over, but he snapped
he yapped
he growled and flapped,
"Damn right I'm pissed."

I tried to apologize, say I didn't mean
to piss him off like that
      "Damn right I'm pissed," he
came back with.
      "Damn right I'm pissed," he
repeated like a damn broken record.

Someone whose opinion I trust suggested
next time I run into him after it's all cooled over
I should try and talk to him.

Any Moron

But I did and he said, "Any moron
could write down a bunch of swears
and call it a poem."
He said, "If you wanna rehash it
we can rehash it."
He repeated, "If you wanna rehash it
we can rehash it."
I said, "I'm not trying to rehash anything
I'm trying to put it all to bed."
So he said again, "If you wanna rehash it
we can rehash it"———like a damn broken record.

Sometimes I say things brash I'll be
the first to admit, sometimes I'm a bit
crude and uncouth and don't take
the feelings of others into consideration
I'll honestly say is true.
But I can't watch my mouth for everyone
I can't censor my words to protect just anyone
It's not my business to coddle you
It's not my business to sit by your bed
and sing a lullaby as you drift off to sleep....

I tried to do the right thing, I tried
I really did
to make things right, but he had
a pig for a head and a bark like a lapdog
so feaux-vicious it made me sad
and he resorted to name calling
resorted to putting me down
because he saw it to be his last resort
maybe his only resort, a comeback
that must have taken the whole weekend to
conjure up.

Jeremy Void

This, from a man more than
twice my age.

I can't please everyone, right??

The Lost Letter

I DON'T WANT TO BE REJECTED
I DON'T WANT TO BE DENIED
I DON'T WANT TO BE HERE AND
I DON'T WANT TO BE THERE

I DON'T WANNA LIVE IN
A WORLD WHERE I CAN'T BE ME
PEOPLE JUDGE BUT THEY DENY
THAT THEY DO
PEOPLE HATE BUT THEY ACT
LIKE THEY DON'T

HYPOCRITES I'M THE BIGGEST ONE
BUT THE THING IS I
DON'T DENY IT AT ALL
I REFUSE TO
I REFUSE TO DO ANYTHING
OTHER THAN WHAT I'M DOING
RIGHT NOW I DON'T LIKE YOU

YOU'RE FAKE BUT SO AM I
YOU'RE TOO LATE AND I
'M THE ONE WHO TAKES THE BLAME
I'M RUNNING WITH THE CROWD
I'M WORSHIPPING THEIR GODD

Jeremy Void

WEARING THEIR CLOTHES
AND TALKING IN THEIR DRAWL

AND NOW YOU WONDER WHY I HATE
MYSELF AND WANNA BASH IN
MY OWN FUCKING FACE YOU WONDER
WHY SUICIDE SEEMS LIKE A SOLUTION
CUZ I'M NOT YOU AND I WOULD RATHER
DIE DIE DIE

DON'T YOU SEE THIS SOCIETY
IS BLIND AND CAN'T SEE NOTHING AT ALL
WE'RE LOST TO THE TV AND THE MOVIES
AND MAGAZINES THAT MAKE YOU STUPIDER
THAN THE FOOLS WHO PREACH ABOUT GOD

I HATE YOU AND YOUR VIEWS
I DISAGREE WITH YOU AND
WHY YOU CHEAT AND LIE AND THROW
IT ALL AWAY I'D RATHER DIE

sounds like the best idea I've heard all day.

Sleepless Beauty

Zzzzzzzzzzzzzzzzzzzzzzzzzzzz....
 Zzzzzzzzzzzzzzzzzzzzzzzzzzzz....
  Zzzzzzzzzzzzzzzzzzzzzzzzzzzz....
   Zzzzzzzzzzzzzzzzzzzzzzzzzzzz....
    Zzzzzzzzzzzzzzzzzzzzzzzzzzzz....

Zzzzzzzzzzzzzzzzzzzzzzzzzzzz....
 Zzzzzzzzzzzzzzzzzzzzzzzzzzzz....
  Zzzzzzzzzzzzzzzzzzzzzzzzzzzz....
   Zzzzzzzzzzzzzzzzzzzzzzzzzzzz....
    Zzzzzzzzzzzzzzzzzzzzzzzzzzzz....

Zzzzzzzzzzzzzzzzzzzzzzzzzzzz....
 Zzzzzzzzzzzzzzzzzzzzzzzzzzzz....
  Zzzzzzzzzzzzzzzzzzzzzzzzzzzz....
   Zzzzzzzzzzzzzzzzzzzzzzzzzzzz....
    Zzzzzzzzzzzzzzzzzzzzzzzzzzzz....

Jeremy Void

If only I was that lucky....
        If only it was that easy....
                If only if only if only
                        I might find a piece of mind....

        But I can't, not in this world.
                It will never happen for me.

Another night spent
        staring at a white wall.
                Another night lost in
                        a brainstorm of creativity....

        But what's it worth
                to drive myself mad like this?

Dance to the Apocalypse

Another wasted day.
Sometimes I don't see the point.
Sometimes I don't care at all.
Sometimes I wanna die.
But sometimes I feel so high and
wanna take your hand and dance
beneath the eyes in the sky.

Let's get crazy, you and I.
Let's go insane, because
we won't live twice.
If we're lucky we'll at least live once
so let's take advantage of
this chance to dance to
the talking sun as it sings a song
of love.

The world is ours, it glistens
beneath the stars, the dance floor
shines and radiates and we'll clickety-clack
till the morning comes, till the sun
comes up and we'll dance
till the world explodes, and we'll
dance until the zombies rise, and
when they do we'll dance amid

Jeremy Void

the walking dead's eating frenzy.

I hear the moon crying.
I see the sky bleeding.
The world has broken apart
and here we are, you and I
me and you, just the two of us
dancing and romancing and living
for the now because that's
all we got to live for anyhow
so let's live for the now
let's celebrate the now

and when it ends
we'll celebrate the then
because the moment will never
fucking end

—not in this lifetime, anyway.

A Hopeless Struggle

It's a struggle
I live in, a fight
I struggle to control
because the fight that
it is has got me under
its control
        and it won't let go.

        It's a hopeless struggle.

I battle its wits, I pull
out my hair before it's too ate
and it's too late for this....
I won't give up, no I won't give up///

I'm living and I'm in trouble
another day another nigh⁻, and it's a fight
not worth the shuffle, but I struggle by
daylight, and the dark of the night, and it
goes **bang**, it goes **bang bang**, and I'm STUCK
and I'm STUCK STUCK FUC<IN STUCKKKKK.

Let me go, I shout.
Let me out, I holler.
Just leave me alone<<< LEAVE ME ALONE....

Jeremy Void

My mental state is at risk
I'm telling you I'm in the midst
of a mental breakdown tearing and biting
and I'm pissed SO FUCKIN PISSED.

This state of mind this state of being
is beating me raw, bleeding me senseless and senseless
and I'M LOSING MY SENSE TO THIS
THIS
THIS FUCKIN BEAST THAT'S IN MY
HEAD, go **bang,** go **bang bang,** and leave
me the fuck alone, go **bang,** go **bang bang,**
and just fuckin let me go, or I'll
go **bang,** go **bang bang,** and splatter my blood
all over THE FUCKIN WALL.

MAKE IT STOP
STOP
STOP

STOOOOOOOPPPP!!!

To Be Seen by You

What do I gotta do to get you
to know who I am?
Who do I gotta fuck to get you
to see me as a man?
Who do I gotta please
who do I gotta see
who do I gotta be
for you to take me seriously?

Come with Me

Disillusioned youth, won't you follow me.
We'll walk hand and hand into the flames.
We'll talk until the moon blows up
make plans to self-destruct.

The joke is broken, it's a caustic day.
The night is smoky, and we're young OK
Let's live for the system and tear it down
Let's die for rebellion and turn it around.

The world is ours and we feel so strong.
Our lives are theirs and we feel so dumb.
Let's go and creep through the streets of hell
We only need something to make us feel.

The land of the free, it's full of sissies.
The home of the brave, it's stuffed with rules
This is America, my friend, where they allow us rights
But they steal our rights so let's go and fight.

They steal our lives so let's go and die....

Futility

I've got nothing to say, but still I'm gonna say it. I've got nobody
 to listen, but still I'm gonna find someone to hear it. Some-
 body will listen whether they like it   or not

and I can assure you
they'll like it

or they won't....

One way or another
they'll hear this poem

if it's the last thing that I do!

I've got nowhere to be, but still I'll find somewhere to go. I've got
 nobody who wants me, nobody who will let me in their
 home, but still——

I will find a house to enter

and I will rob the fuckers blind....

Just wait and see..........................

Jeremy Void

I sometimes ask myself
What's the point of living?

I sometimes tell myself
There ain't no point at all.

What for?   I'll tell you what for

I'm as lost as the next guy
as lost as the last one
he she and me
we all find ourselves lost
........................lost
lost in the supermarket
         as the Clash once said.

The media spun its web
and now we're just
sitting ducks waiting to be
........................dead.......

Just wait and see!

The best we can do
while living is create
something new
         something worth the wait
         something that brings us joy
         something that is better than nothing
         ain't it funny that we've just got
nothing to do   anymore?...

I'm constantly finding myself

Futility

       ....bored
so bored....
so utterly blasé
                (had to use the thesaurus for that one)
sick and tired of the usual
crap.   It's getting old!!!

just like yesterday ...
and the day before....

                It's getting stale

and now we've gotta yell....

Open-Mike at Spring Lake Ranch

Tonight I went to an open-mike
at a fucking hippy farm and all I heard
were songs about love, poems about
absolutely nothing and I got bored
and surely shocked them with my own.

Of course, like always, as is tradition it
seems, my poems were screened before I
went up there, and I was shocked myself
at the leniency Rachel offered me in
screening what I had hand-picked to
read tonight.

I read
    "The Lost Letters: Introduction"
    "A Dreamer, a Schemer, and a Freak" during which I heard
an amplified gasp come from the crowd when I mentioned sucking down the pipe and ramming a spike into one's veins.
    "The Serenade"
    and "A World of Our Own"
all of which will be featured in
my new book called
The Lost Letters.

Open-Mike at Spring Lake Ranch

Then I sat down and was bored
until I got up a second time
to read one more which was
      "Dance to the Apocalypse" a final fuck you before Betsy
drove me and Brian home.

In the car Brian told me
that he had thought
      "A Dreamer, a Schemer, and a Freak"
was a little too much for Spring Lake
Ranch, a hippy farm/treatment center for
drug addicts and spastic people
      ——you know, the crazy ones.

(It's considered a dual diagnosis program.)

Anyway, I did agree with Brian on
that, but Rachel did go through my
large pile of writings and gave me the okay
on all but 3, so I did follow the rules here.

Betsy thought
      "The Serenade"
was a bit too much, and that
I do not see, but everyone has
a right to their own opinion.

This one time, a few years ago,
I found myself in a pickle:
either read
      "The Haunted Bathroom"

Jeremy Void

or the beginning of my memoirs which
I have lost by now and never completed.

A girl I was friendly with, her name is
Joy, suggested I read the memoirs
because it's much more personal, much
more closer to who I am and it gives
people a chance to get to know me.
        Of course, she hadn't
        actually seen the memoirs
        at that point in time

cuz when I read it jaws dropped
eyes widened and I fearlessly
went on to tell all those who sat before
me about the time Kristen stuck a straw
in my ass and poured cocaine through—

and many more war stories weaved in
        all fast-paced, with long run-on sentences
        all triggering, fierce, and oh so in
appropriate for a treatment center/
hippie farm.

Immediately after, Lisa the gardener
approached me in the hallway
and said rather sternly, Never read
anything like that here again.

Although that didn't stop the pleased residents
who laughed at my presentation from
bombarding me and saying how much
they loved it, one girl in particularly was
going on and on and on about how much
she enjoyed it.

Open-Mike at Spring Lake Ranch

(Come to think of it, that might have been
one of the very first things I wrote.)

They had used to screen me before that night
but then they had started to trust me I guess
and then went right back
to screening me after this one reading.

There was this one time when
Josh I think his name was, was
responsible for my traditional censorship
and he said all were inappropriate except one
which he called beautiful.

Honestly I didn't see anything wrong with
any of the poems I had selected that night, unless I
stretched it and I'd have to stretch it far.
The one he did say was appropriate
      "The Flame Dance"
(featured in *Nefarious Endeavors*)
I thought was the least appropriate of the
ones I had chosen to read, and from that
I decided fuck it, this is lame and I'm not
even gonna bother. Fuck Them!!!

So I sat on the living room couch
as performers performed, hands applauded
just watching the second hand move effortlessly
around the face of the clock, the minute hand
moving slower with slight jerks, and the little hand
that represented the hours sit there motionless
and I waited
and waited

Jeremy Void

and waited

went out to have a smoke
but when I came back it was
in the exact same place.

I paced and tapped my fingers
on my legs

until my ride picked me up and
took me home.
    —finally!

But tonight, as I am irritated I have to be
censored like that, I guess I'm grateful for
Rachel's leniency and not telling me no
to everything
        leaving me out in the cold
        like Josh had done.

So   I went up
and read
and at my mention of pipes
and spikes
there sounded a unified gasp
like the whole room inhaled

but I finished strong and there was no
problem at all.

Nobody came up to me and said,
Never read anything like that here again.

In fact, nobody came up to me at all....

Not Enough

It's Not Enough
    It's Not Enough
        It's Not Enough....................

It'll never be enough. One day, some day, soon I hope, I will feel satisfied, but until the day arrives I will seek more of everything, more of **this** more of **that**. The spinning sensation of desiring excess is dizzying and I feel like I might drop plummet and hit the floor hard, but when I do I'll be saying let's do it again.

More more more has been my anthem all my life.

Gimme gimme gimme cuz I need it now.

More more more and I'll never feel satisfied.

I can't get down I can't get down, it's driving me up and down the walls.

A little more of this a little more of that, it'll never end until I'm fucking dead. Until I'm six feet under beneath dirt and grime, but even then I'll be asking for more of that—more dirt and grime, more maggots.

Jeremy Void

Forget about this forget about that. I lived too fast and I've gotta slow down. But this sickness of mine, this ailment that has haunted me all my life, is now opened wide and taking all your ideas, all your suggestions, all your methods to plug this ruthless desire of mine.
But I'll just want more of those. It's no use anymore. Why fight it, why bother trying to survive it, because it will suck me dry and throw me out the window—it's done it before.

Guess I'm just doomed to a life of dissatisfaction, the gloom looming over me like a UFO. I'm sick of the sickness, sick of the pain, but there's just not enough to satisfy me in the end.

It's Not Enough
    It's Not Enough
It's Not Enough....................
Well then I guess I'm fucked. I'm doomed fucked and screwed and I'm running away from the things that I do, the things that I seek, the things that I want, the things that I need, I'm running away but every single turn I make these damn desires always catch up to me———

                                      I want more of the sickness
                                            I want more of the pain

I'm sick of the sickness
I'm sick of the pain

                                         I want more more more
                                              more more more
                                              more more more
                      because It's Just Not Enough........................

An Unstoppable Force

There's not enough
rules & restrictions to hold me down.

There's not enough
waste & neglect to keep me around.

I'll blow a fuse and kick you too,
but only if you're fool enough
to see me do it————————

It's no fun///

i'm alone
i'll always be alone it seems at times....
i'm restless & impatient
i'll always be restless & impatient it seems at times....
the world is broken
& i feel at times   like
        it's my responsibility to put it back together
        like i need to patch it up
        like i need to mend the broken ends
        when
        what i really need is
            to let go
            to put down the rock
            & let
            it mend on its own>>>>>>>>

i feel hopeless
& sometimes i think
    —no, i *know*—
that this hopeless situation is
a terminal reality
        so i run
            & i run far far away
                & i keep running until
                i run outta steam....

It's no fun///

& you kno at times, it's
jus no fun….   It's no fun///

the mess is growing
i'm hibernating, i'm throwing it all away….
life progresses
& i think i'm dying
soon to be completely dead, & it's
jus no fun….   It's no fun///

you kno, this lie
is creeping up behind me
either my time is running out
or i'm jus running outta time….

one way or another, i'm sad
& depleted feeling like this madness
will never come to an end   but it will
                                    it's bound to
                                    & wen it does
you kno, it's
jus no fun….   It's no fun///

i search for meaning
a single drop of sanity
the missing pieces of the puzzle——
lost & broken, or
broken & lost, or
hopeless & exhausted.

it all feels jus the same
like the yellow brick road splits 2 ways
& i stand at the fork in the road
stand there & debate which way to go
but it all seems so hopeless, so

Jeremy Void

i jus turn around & go back home

crawl back into my own skin
& go to sleep   cuz it's
jus no fun....   It's no fun///

i'm LOST. But this world, these circumstances,
don't serve to lead me on my way.
i don't feel belonged
i don't feel accepted
i don't feel like i'm going nowhere
——kicked to the curb
——thrown to the wolves
& nothing ever gets better....

i loved once, but once was too much
for me, for this monster i've grown
to be, a monster who will spit in yr face
but when you're gone miss you dearly
& hit my knees in the lonely, dark corner of my room
& clasp my hands together tightly
        —tighter than they've ever been
        all my life—
& pray for yr return, only to

fall asleep on a tear-soaked pillow
only to dream of a time
a better time, a time when you were here
a time when things were great & happy
& a time i never thought cud end....

but i kno for me, it's
jus no fun....   It's no fun///

Join the Lost

The city sleeps....
We stand on the edge of
the city's mind as it purrs—
Zzzzzzzzzzs arising from its
epicenter. We frolic in the depths
of darkness, a mist billowing up
from the blacktop, a ghostly form
puffing and undulating as it drifts
away in a burst of steam.

We stand here, bored and wasted.
We crave action, something to
happen soon, but if it doesn't come
we'll go the distance to find it
to create it, bring it to life
just to murder it again
& again
............................& again.

This is our life, killing time
and slaying the days with a
second wind that keeps us awake.
it keeps us here and we wanna leave.
nothing is all that this city has
in store for kids like us.

Jeremy Void

We frolic in the deserted alleys
waiting for action but it never
comes to us   and we want it now

so bad....

A Punk Rock Song

There was a day when one
could speak their mind
say what they feel and tell you off
without getting a lecture about it
but I missed that day
and this day I'm here
and today I'm going crazed
and I'll bust up your face.

Don't tell me about it
cuz I don't care
Don't tell me about it
cuz I don't wanna hear it
Don't tell me about it
if you know what's good forya
Don't tell me about it
cuz I'm lost and confused and rearing after you.

There was a day when you could
wear what you want
when you could be what you want
but this day and age freedom is lost
to TV and the Internet and other such devices
and this day and age I'll bust up your face.

Jeremy Void

Don't tell me about it
cuz I don't care
Don't tell me about it
cuz I don't wanna hear it
Don't tell me about it
if you know what's good forya
Don't tell me about it
cuz I'm lost and confused and rearing after you.

An Imperfect Circle

When I was a kid
I sat in class dreaming.
I watched the girls in my school they
came in droves strutting the halls like
demonic angels. I watched them laugh
and frolic, talking in codes
gossiping with their friends whose
eyes glowed fierce.

I tried to talk to them,
but the words were choked.
I tried to talk, but an awkward silence
pooled between us
I tried to speak, really I did,
but my sentences came out
jumbled I stammered and grunted
and they went away
to laugh at the freak with their friends whose
eyes shimmered.

When I was a kid
I watched my classmates
their memories haunting me.
I went home from school every day
just to jerk white tears. My emotions flowed

Jeremy Void

and gushed and I self-loathed like any other
poet who came about
in a treacherous existence like my own.

Then life happened and I grew older
having found escape with substances like
speed and coke and beer and weed and
huffing and dope.
I grew up on those things, bashing and stabbing
my brain with chemicals that
only served to sever my short-term memory.

For girls I lost interest, having adapted
the beautiful line:
> I've got a hand
> to fall back on at night when
> the pretty girls deny my approach
> and kick me to the curb.

I didn't care anymore having
felt the sting of rejection
and I didn't like the feeling one bit.

Nonchalance believe it or not
changed the story
This lack of caring triggered
admission by the pretty young girls who prior
to this laughed and squawked at my advances.
The girls of my desire, and their friends whose
eyes glowed with wonder and enchantment,
mocked me to the end of the rainbow,
where gold cannot be found.

I rode the wand of lust and I didn't care
Fucking girls and exchanging them for a new one
and I didn't care because it was lost on me.

An Imperfect Circle

I got used to the feisty exchange—the meeting of girls
on the subway train and instantly whisking them away
to my private place.

It became normal and I mocked
those who craved tits and ass and pussy
bragging about last night's
enchanted endeavor .... sucking and fucking
and riding the blissful waves of pink pleasure
               to which I was skeptical
                   because I myself
                   did not brag about it
          I did not crave
          I did not care

          The whole pony act was lost on me
          and I did not care

The drugs and alcohol and senseless fucking
really took a toll on me.
I was running from the cops hiding in ditches
my life spiraling out of control
    and I did not care

More life passed me by
I crashed my minivan into a tree
I called my best friend's new girlfriend a cunt
    right to her face
Life was my playground
and I was cocky as can be
fast living and hard music
that brought me to my knees but
I did not care

That was my blessing

Jeremy Void

my burden
impulsive and wild was my curse
which banged me into a gutter
and I did not care

Down there in my gutter
I had girls and drugs and poison that
picked me up and I would never be
knocked down

but I was
and I did not care

I had to stop the insanity
or I'd be shipped off
thrown into the slammer
Hard living would get even harder
and I started to care....

Now I'm back where I started
back from the top
having pulled off the perfect circle
all wound up and destructive

leaving me a wreck who can't talk
to girls if my life depended on it.
My throat gets clogged up
and the words come out all stuttered
and the girls look at their friends whose
        eyes radiate in the sun
           pulsate in the dark beneath the stars
        shine in the heat
        brood in the cold

An Imperfect Circle

and say, *What a freak*

and I go home and jerk white tears again
sad at the failed attempt
at the fact that I'm back where I started
a lost and confused wreck
    I am a freak

    and I do care

The Lost

The nighttime warriors stalk the streets, boots clotting in gutters, stomping through puddles. They stand tall and mean. Black disguises and painted faces. The civilized folk stare but pretend that they don't as the street demons stroll past them and don't even care.

These are the boys

These are the girls

disillusionment run wild. Lost and troubled, they sneer, spit, and scowl. They own these streets——————the night's got nothing they can't overcome.

Seen it all before; been there done that.

From broken homes, broken lives, broken worlds collide, the whole landscape has become their playground, a sandy beach that winds through downtown and swings along uptown, spanning the face of the city, beneath the stars that stretch as far as their eyes can reach....

These are the boys

These are the girls

The Lost

told of in horror stories. The few parents warn their children of, saying these kids are bad, these kids are mean, they will rob you and laugh about it later when they're with their friends.

The boys they don't want their daughters to date

The girls they don't want their sons to fuck

Lives too romantic for the likes of the suburban yuppies. Too wild for the tamed, too mean for the controlled to take. They're menaces, vagrants, young cretins wrecking havoc in this sacred town. The city burning down as these MONSTERS in black clothing come barreling down the road.

These are the kids who live next door, sinister smiles and chains galore. They creep through the city feared by the normal classes. They are doomed to a life of crime, a life of drugs, given up on by just about everyone.

<u>These are your children for whom you turn the other cheek.</u>

So Alone

1.
I sit alone
consumed by shadow
the music like a corrupt soul
oozes and gushes from
some hidden place
           of the mind

2.
the people's chatter
bustling disgusted, and I
feel separated from their
madness
           their
                insanity
                      that
clips me like a hockey puck

3.
the sky is dark
lacking stars—it looks like

So Alone

a big black blanket
        coming down to
        smother me
I look up and see a
pinpoint
        a dot
            one
                green
it lurks in the bleak emptiness
        makes me sad

4.
bodies
they shuffle
        when I look over
        at the giddy hustle
        the people there, scattered
are arranged differently than
the last time I chanced
    a glance
        their way

5.
I wonder—~~sometimes~~
(well, not really)
what the aliens are
thinking about
        what embraces them
        do they crave
        the things that
        make them tick

Jeremy Void

fly off the handle
how can
                I make them pissed
                       >>at me
              if only it was
THAT simple

6.
the painting on the
big brick wall behind
the center street alley
comes to life
              when you look at it just right
                                                  just right

        it peels off the wall
        comes down
            splashes like
            shattering glass
a stark understanding—a dark
      realization, fat and mean
          strong and lean : : : murderous hopeless
                stuck on a futile track
                taking you into the black void—

the last thing on earth that beats
and shines bright like the sun
      churning chemically twisted, and I
decide just now to give up the sickness
and branch out
            if
                only
it wasn't so damn hard

So Alone

and your own heart beat and throbbed
in tune and rhythm with my own
    in unisons
        so for once I could feel whole....
            like an actual human being
            apart of something beyond me
            so that I wouldn't feel so alone
                anymore....

An Outburst at the Beach

At the beach creating
concrete poetry when loud,
angry voices break through
the otherwise happy crowd.

I look right →→ NOTHING

←← I look left
          and I see it
              going down.

Two girls. One guy.
High school age,
maybe freshmen in college.

The two girls are crying now.
The guy's voice is the loudest
of them all, cursing, cussing them out.
The two girls are in the cusps of panic—

                    "Find your own ride home,"
                        the guy spits nastily
                        at his girlfriend's friend.
                            She rushes him
                    gets in his personal space.

An Outburst at the Beach

                                          Eye to eye now, they glare
                                          hard and firm and volatile.

I knew something big was
about to go down—the guy's hands

rocket straight forward
into the girl's shoulders
knocking her back a few feet.

                          Then the girlfriend grabs the keys
              and   storms off.

A spectator bursts in,
a middle-aged woman,
screaming, "You three
get outta here. You're swearing
in front of children.
Leave
    NOW!"—her voice
louder than the guy's
harsher than the two girls'
combined.

The guy storms away
across the beach, straight after
his crying girlfriend who
when I look left is
rounding the bend and vanishing
from my sight.

                and **NOBODY DOES ANYTHING**
        except for the fierce middle-aged woman
            who only escalated the problem
                      [although she does have a point]

Jeremy Void

I see the apathy
and a hot anger seethes inside me—
all the passive actors!

I shout at the table to my right
occupied by three older women
not quite middle-aged but
old enough to have a say—

      "Someone should follow her?"

                                              ... shrugs ...

      "See if she's okay?"

                    ... all the women's eyes look away ...

      "A woman should go after her.
      I can't because I'm a guy
      it'll only make things worst."

                            "Not my business,"
                  one woman says, shrugs,
                          and looks away.

My eyes follow the girlfriend's friend
as she passes the table where I sit,
ascend the steps and disappears where
the bathrooms are. Since I can't see
the doors I don't know if she goes in
    or walks right past.
But regardless I decide to take my chances
and sit on a bench located right outside
      and wait...................

    15 ↓
        20 minutes

An Outburst at the Beach

until she walks out
all teary-eyed and sad.

    "Are you okay?"
    I ask her.

                                        "Yeah"
                                      sniffling
                              "yeah, I'm fine"
                                more sniffling.

    "Are you sure you don't
    want to talk about it?"

                                "Yeah, really"
                   rubbing away the dribble
                    dripping out of her nose
                          "really, I'm fine"
            straining herself
                      to restraint
                                her tears.

                 "Besides," she adds, "I'm
                      waiting for a friend."

                                    Then
             she points straight behind me.
             "There he is," she says with
          a minor hint of relief showing in
                          her tear-soaked eyes.

He walks up the steps, they exchange a tight and sentimental hug,
I say "Good luck," and she says thanks

as they vanish around the corner.

And now all I can think about

Jeremy Void

is the sheer selfishness
the lack of caring
the "It's not my business" feeling shared by

the passive passersby.

It's just sad, is all.

inertia (n)

1. inertness, especially with regard to effort, motion, action, and the like; inactivity; sluggishness.

2. *Physics.*
   a. the property of matter by which it retains its state of rest or its velocity along a straight line so long as it is not acted upon by an external force.
   b. an analogous property of a force: *electric inertia.*

3. *Medicine/Medical.* lack of activity, especially as applied to a uterus during childbirth when its contractions have decreased or stopped.

I'm sitting in the shadows
in the dark corner
behind the Alley.

I'm bored and tired
crazed and wired
> the fumes seeping through
> my pores like smoke

I'm cold and sad
so alone and lost
my mind stretched like
a rubber band pulling out
> thoughts
> one after another

and then it snaps
and all these fleeing ideas
like crystalized dreams
cram into my head, jammed up tight
overflowing
> the lost ponderings

Jeremy Void

                filling me up
                like pollution///

the toxic gas exploding my head
making me mad and I might just
      snap
         in half————wouldn't you
                like that?

I'm scared holding onto
        hopeless fantasies
the world rolling like waves
going topsy turvy curving and swerving
            swirling
and I try to hold on to
the walls, but they——————————————————
      collapse
      and I'm back
      where I started
      back from the top
      unable to withstand the static
      the rapid flipping///

This whole world is
tipping
      dropping into
            oblivion.

I'm scared searching for
      some kind of salvation to
wrap me up in its
      hospitable madness
the talons scratching me
      and I let go————
      the floor drops out

inertia (n)

       from beneath me

and I didn't expect it
to happen quite like
this………………………..

I'm scared and sick
horrified and pissed
          or maybe

          it's just emptiness.

I fill the relentless emptiness
with dastardly things——
          things that make me
          see things I don't wanna
          see

          but it's too late….

for me>>>>>>>

At the Top of the World

the world
blotted out with bliss
We run in the skids
frolic & rip off our skins.
    We are great
    We are tall
    We run amok & we run
with all the kids\\\

The past is missing its prowl.
The future is livid & sour.
The present is big too big to devour.
We mustnt hide we mustnt let go.
We must stand our ground &
we must fight for what's ours.

The world is burning down around us
Buildings flicker in the night.
We rob & steal   thieving & killing.
We thrive on death & death
prospers in life.

The end is nigh. The end is coming.
The meaning is lost & the beginning
    is found

At the Top of the World

      found
          found. We watch the bird//
The bird it flies & swoops & dives.
We see it kill & hunt & hunt & kill.
The orange sun shines down around us.

& I say to myself, It's a good day
          to die!

No Comment

Tooooo much going on
& I just can't relate.
This life is killing me
and my fate is screwed
——up....

The only way is up
but I'm stuck in a downward
spin that's taking me to
yesterday and tomorrow is just a dream.

My mind stops the swirl
my brain is twirling
making me dizzy and it won't
let up the spin is sick and it's
sickening me to shitttttt.

I don't know what I want....
Am I supposed to?
I know what I don't want,
but what I don't want is you
and you just won't go away....

Censor Censorship

The problem with censorship is

The bookstore wouldn't sel my books
because families and chilcren come to
their precious little store.

Art in the Park picks and chooses
who they allow in.

The problem with censorship is

There's just very little art in this world
that I myself enjoy.

Because the rough art gets weeded out
the clean art gets weeded in and that's
not what I came here to see.

Censor nothing I say.

I want the right to choose
what I see
        don't you?

Jeremy Void

I want the right to decide
what to believe
········don't you?

I want to have control over
the content filtered into my mind
I want to decide what gets
featured in my conscious.

Censor censorship I say.

My thoughts are my own and I want
total control over my mind and what
I feed it with.

I want rough art because the clean art
says nothing and means nothing and it seems
so pointless to me.

Censorship ought to be a crime.

Barely Alive

Another night with no sleep.
Drenched in sweat, haven't bathed in a week.
I feel sick and twisted and
full of caffeine.
I might be manic, but then it's all just a dream.

The story unfolds with lots and lots
of sadness that evolves into
lots and lots of badness that evolves into
crashing and burning, the wall breaks my
fall.

I sometimes hate my past, but then when
I think back on it and remember
all the good times I had, I put my fist
through the mirror
cuz I hate the present so fucking much——

so much it will destroy me!

Life was better in another age, another
time, another state, another place far
far away from here, and 'll do anything I can
to put myself there—like drink Nyquil, for one.

Jeremy Void

Walking on the edge, testing the waters,
I'm a ticking time bomb set for
destruction mode, and I will explode all over
the walls in

my own personal hell.
Just wait and see....

My world revolves around me.
It's all I see when I look
in the Godforsaken mirror which
never shows me what I wanna see.

Life, sadness, craziness, it's all insane.
Life, happiness, blissful living, it's just a lie.
Disillusioned and wild, I thrive on it
the phony world masking the real one
I woke up years ago and I just want to
go back to sleep.

But another night wide awake makes me
see a side of life you only see in dreams.

The Light Will Do That to You

I look straight ahead.
Turn left they said.
Turn left or right just
don't go into the light.

The light it shimmers with ominous might
I stare into the translucent beam that cuts a straight line
through the world, benches and parking meters
and tables flipping and tumbling as the beam
plows a bleak path that feels quite inviting
      to me.

I look left and
my family stands there waving.
I look right and
my childhood friends stand there glaring
chiding me along with beckoning hands.

The light shines bright with mischief
with mystery and romance
To my left and right is familiar ground
the ground on which I've walked time
and time again and frankly
I'm so bored of the monotony.

Jeremy Void

I take one steady step forward—
        silence spreads
        like a dispersing mist
        encompassing my friends
        and family as they stare
        in complete and utter suspense.

Another step and I feel
a quiver sliver up my spine.
A nervous jitter wound with an
exciting glimmer in my eyes—another step!
The ground rumbles….

I take another step
Then I hear voices again as I take
another step, and then another….
Voices telling me I'm going the wrong way
    that way is dangerous
    I can get hurt
    come and play with them
    follow them as they tread
    on familiar ground
    doing routines day after day
    and wasting away my life
    just waiting to die

I keep on walking toward the light
the inviting glow that shone from the rip in the fabric
a *real* beckoning force that was too strong to resist
and <u>then I was there</u>
    <u>took a questioning glance at my rear</u>
    <u>saw what I was leaving behind me</u>
    <u>saw the horror that rose from the sleeping souls</u>
    <u>and I realize at the moment</u>
        <u>there's no turning back</u>

The Light Will Do That to You

I hurry up the three steps
as an epic gasp comes from my friends
and family—NOOOOOOOOOOO!!!!

I stop there
stop in place
my feet planted and spread on two separate steps
twist my waist, cock my head,
screw up my face, and an electric middle finger
springs into place.

A final fuck you before

the light embraces me and I never
felt more alive.
The world was flaming and there were kids
wild and running and knocking things down.
One kid waved at me, motioned me over.
I took a look over my shoulder as the hole
sealed up and the damage was done
I was here <u>THERE WAS NO TURNING BACK</u>

My Cocaine Cherry

The first time——

Huddled in a McDonald's bathroom
somewhere on this planet
I sat on a toilet with a tray on my lap,
sprinkled that beautiful white powder
on the tray, took a credit card and molded
it into lines.
I rolled a dollar bill and stuck it in my nose
lowered my face over a line and
sucked
pulled the cocaine in——

                a blast of white lightning
                 a blast of adrenaline
                a blast of cocaine biting
                a defibrillator to my brain
                              and I was good to go....

I lifted my head.
Stars, bright and vicious
shone in my eyes.
I felt fabulously twisted.

I stood up....

My Cocaine Cherry

The whole world was mine
I could do anything
anything
        anything
                !!ANYTHING!!

I stood up
left McDonalds
and the sky looked so sweet
so beautiful
the magical stardom   the air on my face
the bleak nothingness overhead
I did a B-line for the street

                (this is my first time)

and found somewhere to sit
behind a restaurant
somewhere on this planet
and I sat
and sat
and sat lying there
and stared up at
the stars as they painted arrays
of magic and delight up in
the black sky

it was brilliant
it was scary
it was magnificent
it was horrifying

something was going on in
my head
something great

Jeremy Void

something sad
something wonderful
something bad....

> (they say
> your first time is
> the best time and after that
> it's just chasing dragons)

I never wanted to come down
the world was mine and I
felt the power
radiating deep
in my veins///

I was Super Man
I was Wonder Woman
I could scale vertical walls
just like Spider Man
or run as fast as a speeding bullet
like the Flash
chasing after busses and trains....

I sat on the ground
I sat and I watched the sky
     relaxed
I was relaxed
and I felt ecstatic.

Blitzed and wired
crazy and wild
I could take on the world
I could take on my life
and things would never

My Cocaine Cherry

ever

be the same again....

———DAY 1———

———DAY 2———

———DAY 3———

———DAY 4———

———DAY 5———

———DAY 6———

and I'm crashing.
I think I'll go to sleep.

Wake me up when
you obtain another graham
of this magical white lightning

because the world
in comparison
      just ain't worthy of
my presence///

What You Need to Know

My goal isn't to bore you
It isn't to make you numb
You're dumb and that's your problem
My writing is not a drug.

It will not lift you up
It will not make you high
You might wanna die
But that's your problem, not mine.

A Pit of Despair

A Pit of Despair—
i sit in this hole—my hole—its what im used to, having become familiar w/ this hole which i typically occupy alone, having no room in it for outsiders—its just me & this cavernous hole, & sometimes i stare up at the sky from inside my hole, watching the planes soar overhead, clouds billowing & floating in space—& at night the stars dot the sky like freckles, the moon big like a volleyball—its proof enough that theres something more, beyond what the eye can see, a beauty interspersed w/ rotting death clinging to the atmosphere, beyond what our eyes can read—& so i wonder why i ended up here, in this shell, this hole, a useless body no good for nothing—the stars like glitter upset me because they feed me the knowledge that there is in fact beauty (*actual* beauty) in the world, only there is no beauty in this hole, just a wasted soul, solely the cause-and-effect of years after years of mindless self-destruction—it really took a toll on me, you know—

i found love & i lost it. i had friends but now theyre dead————— or alive, one or the other it dont make a difference to me—all i know is that theyre not here & i sit in this hole, my hole, a futile existence that is me, my life unfolding to reveal more & more misery that will spin around me, lapping me as if running a race, right around my head, wrapping me in guilt & shame & these things called inhibitions—whoever thought of that **must** be shot, because inhibited is a restricted form of living whereas uninhibited, mostly

Jeremy Void

caused by a drunken or drugged-up state, will wake the dead & put them to rest—& beside all that, art must be done from an uninhibited standpoint or else your connection to your muse gets intercepted & you lose him—sometimes for good

sometimes i question the reasons i try, the reasons i push myself forward—this incessant excuse to stay alive & healthy is eating me up, beating me raw, & my motivation to do anything is sinking into oblivion so that soon ill stay stagnant in my hole, unmoving as life ricochets & bounds & rushes & hurries thru time & my time ceases

i stay in my hole not knowing a single soul—& its lonely down here—& i cud certainly use company, anyone wanna come over for dinner sometime?—yeah, i know, theres only one of two foreseen outcomes to that: bore my guest senseless; or sicken him to death, make him spew, lift his head from the sink, turning it slowly & in disbelief, a deep grimace engraved in those crud-stained lips, & call me a *freak* right to my face—& then off he goes, to never be seen or heard from again.

they say life is short, enjoy it while you can—my life, having recently turned 28, has gone on way too long & i wudnt mind a climax soon: a stray bullet, a fire, an overdose (no way, i dont do drugs anymore—hint hint   wink wink), or something so i can finally see how my time ends, so the anticipation of the inevitable stops nagging at me, my imagination running haywire as it fabulously crafts a grid that depicts the rest of my life, every move i make until i die outlined & grafted on the biggest sheet of paper youd ever see (its called the brain)....   —but in case there are any newcomers reading this, i must add that my imagination is typically off by a longshot, every single time—always shoots too far left or right, or the horseshoe wizzes past the pole & curves & comes down, clomping on the grass & sand.

A Pit of Despair

if i had to pick one outcome, one path to go on, if i had all the capabilities as the average human being (because im just a mongoloid hole-dweller, dont you know?)—i mean anything—what wud i do?—id probably climb out of this hole & get on w/ my life, leaving my brooding behind in the dirt where id come from.

(Truth be told, I'm not really such a miserable person, and although my poetry and prose might seem rather dark and depressing to you, I can assure you I'm typically a very pleasant person................
But on another note, I might not be as pleasant in **real** life if I didn't have this poetic outlet that allows me to rant and rave and insult the world in my own beautiful poetic style, coming across as ungrateful and mean. I know where I was, and I know where I am, and I can assure that I am very grateful and I will never forget, but part of me is pushing my more reasonable side to forget it all and devolve back to my old self-destructive nature which I though I had capped up and thrown into the back of my car many years ago.))))

i want out of this **hole**
i want out of this **hole**
i want out of this **hole**
!!!NOW!!!

Pledge Allegiance to ... what?

I'm lost in a corrupted world
in a broken society
in the land of the free
the home of the brave
        or so they say.

I'm lost in tomorrow's world
in yesterday's society
in the land of the broke
the home of the pompous
        or so they preach.

I'm stuck in this twisted world
in an assbackwards society
in the land of the fat
the home of the _____
        I'm going to sleep....

Redemption

The kid at Store 24 kicked
me down and knocked me out
played basketball with my head
screaming he's gonna fuckin
kill me dead.

The gang of hoodlums surrounding me
at the train station because ... why? ...
I ripped somebody off
I ratted somebody out
I rattled somebody's chain and now
I was about to pay
and it wasn't going to be pretty.

The kid who I had called a friend
who had left a ladder of scars up my shins
with the toes of his boots.
The two fuckers who cornered me around
the swingset and I took a fierce
uppercut to my stomach. It dropped me.

My brother and friends—the pounding
they served to me.
My brother attacking me while I slept
attacking me cuz my alarm clock was relentless

Jeremy Void

woke him up and I stayed asleep
woke him up and this made him mad
woke him up and he clobbered me as
I Slept.

The cops throwing me and company
against the wall because ... we were there?
Threatening us trying to get us to serve
the first strike.   The cops who showed up at
the window of the truck and took us in
———possession of cocaine they said.

Why did it all happen to me?
I didn't deserve that kind of strife.
I didn't deserve that kind of life.
I didn't deserve to be treated like
the fucking enemy ...
            but I was....

and I swore to make them pay—

The guy who forced himself
on my girlfriend took a knife to
the side of his neck and then
a series of misguided slashes all across
his face.

The cars I fucked up, the property
I destroyed, the people I hurt....

The people I hurt....

Was it worth it? Revenge can very well
feel good and well, especially when the
knife rips through a layer of skin

Redemption

and blood spurts through the wound.

From knife fights to fist fights
to fires to broken glass
to tires exhaling and my own knuckles
gushing
blood.
From black eyes to bruised and swollen lips
to scabs and scars and broken bones

I did it all. And now
I wonder if these cunts today ever
knew the boy that I was
        (pulling a krife on high schools kids
          and saying the red dye on my girl's hands
          was really blood)
would they respect me?
        (stealing a pocketbook out from under
          the back of a seat at the movie theater
          and making a good $200)
or would they fear me?

You'd think, in life, doing the right thing
would make your life better.
You'd think, in life, being a better person
would heighten your chances of happiness
of a happier outcome.

You'd think....

Same shit different day, people ripping on me
and I wanna take em
I wanna take em
take the fuckers and rip cut
their fucking eyes and then

Jeremy Void

fuck em through their fucking sockets.
Wouldn't that be nice?

I assure you I am a better person.
No more ripping off the helpless old lady
no more stealing and cheating and lying through
my teeth—it's all behind me
that life
that style
that way
—I'm good now and I do
good things, but I'd never miss the
opportunity to gun down the cunts
who take me for granted.

I walked through hell
and survived.
I met the devil face to face
and lived to see another day.
I sold him my soul for a six-pack
and a bag of crack, but
fuck that red-faced prick
cuz you bet I stole it back.

That's my life
that's my story
I'm a better person now but that
doesn't change the fact that I
got these sick thoughts coursing
through my head
doesn't change the fact that
I wish you were dead.

Suffering

I wanna get high,
but I don't.
I wanna have a life,
but I won't.
Living feels cold and depressing
and I want instant relief but
the only kind of relief I ever get
ties me up and beats me
with long bamboo sticks as trippy
midget demons prance around me in loin cloths
praising Jesus Christ ... and I'm scared.

The Streets aren't safe

"I disapprove of what you say, but I will defend to the death your right to say it."

— Evelyn Beatrice Hall

Leftist Nazis
        everywhere
swarming the streets.
They fly their banners
        like Gestapo
berating those who refuse
to live by their rules.

The mob has spoken
ruled in favor of PC.
They have us outnumbered.
The Streets aren't safe
        no more....

Running scared———
They've got the numbers
They've got the laws
in their favor
        everyone is following
        the New World Order.

I hang out with

The Streets aren't safe

the REAL social deviants
the kids like me and you.
We hold the truth
in our hands.

The mob is beating down on us
like a stampede tearing through the wilderness
cutting like a knife
cold as ice—their flags
their banners
their systematic justice
the wars they wage
on intolerance.

The Streets aren't safe
        no more.

We hide in our homes
silenced and afraid.
Well we have a voice too
We've got something to say to you.

Hunted like Jews
in World War II
Burned on the stake
like faggots
in the Salem Witch Trials

Muffled and oppressed
they shut us down
they shut us up
they kick us out
they just don't want us around.

What happened to the days

Jeremy Void

of Free Speech?
cuz all I want is an America
where I have the right
to be me
a world where I can speak
······openly and freely
············and unopposed by the likes of

....*YOU*....

A World of Our Own

I feel cold.
I want you to warm me
in yours arms
hold me tight and tell me lies
about a better place
a place where even the misfits
fit in.

I need encouragement
Will you nourish me?
Pull me close and whisper dearly
about a world where even you and I
could be king, a world where the winners
lose and the losers thrive.

What do I gotta do to
get you to hold me?
What lies must I tell you
to get you to coddle me
to squeeze me in your arms
and tell me
it'll be alright.

Everything's gonna be fine.

A RANT, so to speak

A RANT
A RANT—where do I begin?
Maybe start from the simplest abstraction
      and move out from there
a mega expansion of the conscious mind
a light to shine down on it—
      OK here I go....

For two nights in a row
I stayed awake in
my steaming apartment—driving
myself insane just
so I can write more—manic
and whacky I started to see things
like bugs trilling about
so I had to go out before I
ripped out my eyes—just to
stop me from seeing.

Now I'm down the street, on
a couch in someone else's living room.
Whose house? you might be asking....
It's a halfway house I used to live in
and I'm known
to cruise down here from

A RANT, so to speak

time to time, drink there coffee
as I chillax and read on their
comfy couches.

But the problem is
now I'm being charged for
my visits—not like I
don't pay a shit-ton of money
just to be in this program to begin with.
Well, my parents pay
        and I hate that
          I'm embarrassed
they get the fee when I
overstay my visits at this
goddam halfway house
        and I hate that
          I'm embarrassed
and yet
I continue to reap the awful rewards
of being a burden.
I continue to cruise down the block
and pop my head in Royce St.—that's
                       what we call it
                       anyway
for a visit and a chance at
"free" coffee.

Sure, I could leave this program
cuz that would surely make a difference
and my parents could go on
that dream vacation they'd been planning
ever since I was stranded
here
in the first place

Jeremy Void

at first it was that hippy-dippy farm
called Spring Lake Ranch
and then—the second largest city
in all of Vermont, with
the most bars per capita in all of
the United States of America
                    —that
                        just to get sober
                        I know, ain't
                        it a joke?

Anyway, this rant has digressed
and now
I'm back on track.

This dream vacation which my father
denies the existence of, like he
never imagined a world in which his
middle son wasn't such a fuckup
such a burden
and he could have been
filthy rich and fly all over
the freaking world—but the truth of the matter
is
I'm just a burden
sucking the family dry.

So why not leave?
Cuz I'm scared to—I'm
horrified of the prospect of
not having this safety net
        someone to catch me
        when I fall
                and I know
                my legs are just aching

A RANT, so to speak

        to give
        and let me go crashing
        face-first into
        that black market drug store
        right around the corner—
you know the one

So I'm in a bind.
I'd ask you to help me
out of it
but I'd rather not
suck my parents any dryer than
I already have
     and I hate that
       I'm embarrassed
but it's a matter of fact

and I'm not in the practice
of fabricating pretty bullshit for you
     or for anyone….
bullshit you can hold
and pet
and kiss
and bring home

but then it explodes
and you see it for what
it really really is
just a stinking log of shit
and to think you actually
put it in your mouth
believing the lies that
it was just a goddam Toblerone
     a piece of shit disguised
     as chocolate

Jeremy Void

I'm not that devious
I'd rather—in reference to me anyway—
tell you
exactly
how it is....

and if you don't like it
would rather eat shit
then good riddance you
deserve nothing more.

Anyway
this rant is wrapping up now
just closing up tight
and locking me
out——to never
be seen
again.

Good fucking riddance for that....

A Dreamer, a Schemer, and a Freak

A true poet—

To be a true poet
one must walk in death's shadows
one must see the truths and learn how to spin
magnificent lies

The poet treads on the outskirts
always on the outside looking in
sometimes envious but usually
dallying in the realm of the narcissist

To be a poet
one must not forget anything
no single detail of guilt and shame
lost in a brainstorm of historical facts

The poet finds love in loveless entities
sucking down the pipe and ramming the spike
into his veins, tipping bottles and running scared
all the time. The poet thrives on misery

prospers in pain, usually self-inflicted
an existential, twisted thing that most people avoid
but for the poet it becomes god

Jeremy Void

his soul purpose
the only reason to go on

The poet's life is a lonely one
a pondering so deep it alienates himself
the poet is born to lose
a rebel with no cause, a writing devil
that spins fabricated psalms for you
and then erases them in a wisp of flames
because it will never be good enough

Solitude is the poet's only destiny
he squanders alone and searches
for someone to whom he can relate
but like everything else in the poet's life
his search turns up no results

The poet is a thief stealing hearts
stealing you but too detached to move
his own heart, it just throbs with toxic emotions

The darkness comes and the poet
sits alone in the shadows with
his pen and paper and scribbles a note
to himself:

    Was it worth it?

Your Problem Is Your Problem

If you've got a problem with me,
rest a sure
it's your own problem/
I can't spend the greater part of
my days worrying about whether
I impressed you/
I can't worry about if what I said
fell in line with your core values
with your core beliefs—cuz it's
a waste of time/

This is my life, and I'm the one
in the driver's seat—no one appreciates
a backseat driver, someone who tries
to steer my life in the direction they deem
fit

cuz only I know
the right way to go....
only I know the right path
that suits me, cuz I am me>>>>>>>>
      not you
      not he or she
      but me
This is my life and only I

Jeremy Void

know what's right
         for me/

I can't waste my time worrying
about whether I offended you
worrying about your problems, cuz I've got
my own problems, problems that
I created on my own accord....
I can't cater to your feelings anymore
than I can cater to his hers or the tranny
in the corner's///

Sinfulness Is Godliness

Sins are good
sins are great
The God we believe in
is all for vices.
He says
kill the wife
Kill the children
All is good as long as
you kill someone.
Steal rape and get fat
cuz all is good in God's land.
Fight others of different creed.
Beat them down and make em bleed.
Sinfulness is godliness
or at lease that's what the Bible says.

In Search of the Truth

The answers are escaping me.
These truths or so they claim
have got me wrapped up
in a blanket of lies.

All I want is the truth.
It's all I've ever wanted
all I've ever seeked
AND to get it I'll
do just about anything.

Steal cheat and lie
just to get by
just to get the answers
to see past your lies   lies that are

burning me up, beating me raw.
Lies that twist me inside out
and pelt me till I'm black and blue
with a long bamboo stick....

I'm sick and confused.
I'm startled and bemused.
I'm lost in a blundering hellhole
these lies swirling up past me

In Search of the Truth

like a rising tornado tearing things apart
tearing me down
tearing out my eyes   cuz I don't
wanna see it anymore.

Why bother trying when
the whole world is a lie?
Why proceed when the people
    that I know
are only steering me wrong, pointing me to
a dead end and it's the only way
    to go....
The only way out of here

that I know.

Lost in a Sequence of Screams

RUN!!!! I found myself running and I ran for my life. The cars and the ferries chased after me and the river ran alongside, spewing fish that rose and bent and dipped and dove back into the black water that splashed and flowed and whirled and rose up as the approaching hill hit me like a hurricane—and I stopppppped!

<u>My eyes open. Pitch black. Everywhere. I flail searching panicking—where am I? I roll and squirm, and my upper body rises up and I thump my head on the steel plate that runs across the ceiling boards. Phew, I'm just at camp.
My head swims as I allow myself to fall back asleep....</u>

The sirens tore and wavered. I was being chased by bats, they swarmed me and they swirled and they ate at me and I was over the gate and charged the subway I'd be safer down there. The subway car beat into the station, smashing out of the tunnel, a large flutter of lighting immersing the whole ramp on which I stood. Darkness to light.
The wind picked up and billowed past me.
The train thundered and stopped, the doors slid open, and I turned and saw the flock of bats roaring down the trail. They swirled in a zigzagging form, and I slipped through the door, praying that they shut before the bats caught me here.

Lost in a Sequence of Screams

Then the doors slid together, becoming a solid wall with a rubbery window that wobbled and undulated as bat after bat rammed into it and blood splashed and stained the rubber.

The train was off. I watched the flock of bats conjugate on the ramp, moving and crisscrossing each other, wings flittering as they came together to form a wavering skull. It watched me leave, all dark and menacing-like.
The right eye winked at me just as I fully vanished from their sight.

In the rush of everything I slowed my breathing some and dallied over to find a seat. The guy beside me wore a raincoat with his hood flipped up. He carried a cane in his … *skeletal hands.*
No fucking way.
I looked at him just in time to see his head turn and there was only darkness in his hood with two bright red orbs getting brighter as they bore into me.
I jolted to my feet, stumbled back, nearly tripped, but caught myself, as this creature stood up and started toward me. Nowhere to go. I pressed my back to the wall cringing in fear, my body recoiling as he moved in, and there was just nowhere to go….

YOU, he buzzed at me, thrusting his cane. YOU!!!!

The lights in the train fluttered off, and when they came back on there was a mannequin standing there and its head was melting. Blood pouring out of the disintegrating statue that was once….

I tapped the door, tapping it, praying that it would let me off soon, just let me out, and with an inhale the door released and I fell through the opening

straight through, my arms recoiling like a whip as I tried to grab hold of something

Jeremy Void

but it was too late
i was falling ...

screaming

falling

flailing

falling

screaming and flailing into
blackness ...   darkness

<u>I bounce once, twice, open my eyes, and I'm in bed. I'm panting
with harsh, manic breaths, my heart rattling in my chest, and I try
to calm myself down, saying it was only a dream again and
again—breathe in breathe out.
It was only a dream. A dream. I check my watch and I have 6
hours to go before breakfast.
I set my head gently on the pillow and....</u>

My heart ricocheted in my chest, something was wrong, terribly
wrong; I ripped the covers off me....
but I was stuck they were holding me down.
I squirmed and pushed and twisted and bobbed, forcing my head
out the top. But whatever it was wouldn't let up, trying to suffo-
cate me beneath my comforter. I pushed against it, jamming my

Lost in a Sequence of Screams

head through until I saw the tiniest glimmer of light, the moon reflected off a jagged crack in the bedside window. That crisp sliver, stabbing through the glass like a bolt of lightning, somehow renewed my dwindling strength. With all the might I could muster I shoved my head straight through. It emerged from under the covers. I lifted it straight up, it rose tugging the rest of me along, but I couldn't move my arms ... or my legs. I squirmed but it was no use. The comforter deformed into slime, dripping green goo and up and around came these big gooey tentacles thrashing and coming down on me ...

but

I slipped through the bed
and landed on my feet and was off running again.

Dodged a bright blue minivan whose horn honked at me. I spun and jumped out of the path of a shiny blue BMW. Lights flooded the street I was on....

Cars from every direction.

I was jumping and weaving, cars were honking and closing in, headlights flickering and climbing the walls of the tunnel which rolled like gears clinking and clanking and catching me in their spin and I was stammering up the walls, like a hamster in a wheel, and when I looked left I saw an actual hamster in a wheel, its squat, furry legs scurrying toward me as I ran.
Ran away.
The hamster was getting closer. Gaining speed. I was running, trying to run faster, but I was only spinning my wheels in the tunnel as the gears spun round and round and I followed it like a treadmill moving at its own pace, but the hamster wheel was gaining on me and I couldn't go any faster. It was gaining speed, and rolling quick and wobbly as the hamster's legs kicked and jabbed and I

Jeremy Void

kept running as the thing was coming at me faster and faster and faster faster ... break crash shatter
I dove out of the way, landing on my side, flipped onto my back, and looked up and ...

holy fuck....

A giant sword was coming down like a pendulum, and I rolled out of its path. When it hit the ground, there sounded a metallic clang, and a hailstorm of sparks rose up, spiderwebbing through the air.

I was tired, I needed to catch my breath for a moment. I panted, lay there, hoping the worst of it was over

        when I saw it——*a fucking spider.*

It descended the orange and red ember-like web which pulsated with vivid spiraling colors that rolled up and down the strands. The spider, too, pulsed and throbbed like the sun, its eggsack yellow and ready to burst.
I backed up slowly, not wanting to alarm the hairy, eight-legged beast. I crab-walked away, not averting my eyes for fear of what it might do outside of the spotlight.
Its hairy legs worked out of sync as it maneuvered itself smoothly across the web.
I crab-walked
Its dicers clicked and clacked as it traversed the web and headed straight to something that had gotten tangled up in the sticky strands.
I crab-walked
Effortlessly it punctured the tangled thing with a wooly mammoth-like tooth, blue blood sprouting as the thing flattened and depressed like a deflating balloon.
I crab-walked

Lost in a Sequence of Screams

The spider spun around and faced me.
I crab-walked
Its yellow eggsack pulsed in greater throbs now.
Like a deep inhalation
and a deep exhalation, again and again.
I crab-walked

and then the yellowish sack erupted. Missiles sailed straight from the sack and they hit the gray sky one at a time, sending out miraculous firework blasts; with each blow the sky rumbled and quaked, rippling like a blanket being pelted with wind. The missiles multiplied into a thousand smaller missiles rounding the sky like darts honing in on their targets, and then popping and clattering when the time was right, and even smaller missiles emerged from the pops, curving and spiraling in a siderweb-like design—

Shit, a rickety skitter was coming closer.

I looked toward the tittering sound, and a million spiders were coming toward me, like an army of them. I forced myself back, a twisting crab-walk of a thing that turned me right around and my arms were pumping as I made a break for the river.

I risked a glance behind me and the mama spider stood tall and proud behind its many fledgelings, moving with the flow, almost as if riding on their backs but that was not the case because I saw one wiry, hairy leg rise up as if spring-loaded, the leg unfurling and spreading long across the sky, and then it curled, folded, and came back down; the ground shook and knocked me off my balance as an eruption lifted a cluster of spiders and each one snapped out of existence like a firecracker—I stumbled to regain my balance. Steadied myself. My legs spread apart, I looked at the mama spider, at its wide, murderous, red-lipped grin, and into its sharp, striking eyes

Jeremy Void

and I swear

>time stopped, and I saw myself in a labyrinth that spun around and around, all axles on every side lifting and shifting and coming down to block me in.

>Zoom in. I saw myself in a padded cell, in a straightjacket lolling about the room, rolling from one wall to the next, and I heard the laughter ... that laughter

that knocked me from my stupor, and the spider stood tall amid the approaching swarm, its back arched and its mouth gapingly wide to allow the laughter that surged up from its throat. It materialized in an array of different colored bubbles—blues and greens and purples and pinks thats popped and played a different laughing note.

I whirled and made a dash for the river. It was getting nearer. I saw it there and leapt into the air, flying right over the beach, and in one flowing, coiling motion that brought me straight to the water swished into it, straight and penetrating, my body bending as the river sent me straight down.
I flapped my legs and paddled my arms, turning around in the clear blue stream, and then gazed straight up as billions of tiny spiders skated over the water.

When the last one vanished over the bend and there was no sight of the mama spider anywhere, I kicked up and swam to the surface, pushing and treading water with my feet. My head surfaced soaking-wet, as I took in a much-needed breath.

Then a blast of red flames washed over me—

Lost in a Sequence of Screams

<u>My eyes flutter open. I surface in the dark, flailing for some sort of resemblance to tell me where I am.</u>
<u>Shit shit shit—I squirm in my covers, roll over onto my stomach, head level with the window, and I see the sun shining and my campmates conjuring around the firepit.</u>
      Breakfast time. Thank God.

On Picking Sides

Someone said we must
pick sides and I think, to be
honest picking sides is shit.
So I replied with, If
two friends are bickering do you
pick sides or try to find a solution?
YOU CANNOT COMPARE A REAL
LIFE SITUATION WITH A SILLY ANALOGY
LIKE THAT ONE—anarchy 101, she
said.

She said I don't get involved
She said I'm apathetic
my way of thinking is bullshit
I'm wrong
I'm wrong she said.
You've gotta GET INVOLVED....

Surely I do, but surely I do.
I think we should all get involved.
Surely I do, but surely I do.
But is picking sides really the answer?
Or does it cause more turmoil?—
the very thing we are trying to avoid.

On Picking Sides

It takes two to tangle
It takes two to wage war
If sides are dished then barriers
are torn and when barriers are torn
you can be damn sure that that
means war.

Let's get involved
Let's speak our minds
but not cuz we're smarter
because no we are not.
We are no more than them
they are no more than us.

So let's get involved and
try and find the answers.
Let's help our fellow man
but not because we are better
because surely we are NOT

We are human and we know no more
than any other human
because I'll say it again

we

are

human, and we

know no more
than any other

——and that's all I know.

Words That Heal

If I could say anything
just one thing
to tear into your mind
rip through your soul
beat your heart before it beats you

If I could spell it out
turn the world around with
the perfect words
which will lift you up
and twirl you
hurl you into the stars

When the night is right
and my mind buzzes
frightened disgusted lost
I sometimes have it there
bring it here
spit it out and it always
comes out sound
so sound
it goes way over my head

If I had the perfect words
the perfect verse

Words That Heal

a line to save the world from itself
to change your mental health
to rip you open
lick you and suck you
and fuck you till the world melts

If I could speak to you so softly
that you would bleed for me in a coffin
rotting in the ground like a dirty crown
wrapped around your head, wrapped
in barbed thorns that stab you deep
deep in the brain

If I had the magic words that could
bring about change
the perfect rhyming line
that would end all war
end all fighting, all famine

perfection at its very worst

If I had those characters
the symbolic English letters
that would heal you

I might just stop writing....

Little Derelict

A cacophony
a cocoon I sit in
the disarray
it wraps me up and tries
to smother me down.

I'm innocent. I'm bright.
Will I survive the night
without trying to start a fight?
I don't know, I'm lost
falling into your arms.
You'd catch me, but then you'd
drop me, kick me, hit me
till I bleed.
I'd plead for you to stop
but to be honest
I kinda like it
makes me feel nice and raw
like an animal in the wrong.

I creep behind the city
in the backstreets, lingering in
derelict taverns.
These are my people, but
they hate me, but

Little Derelict

they don't know me, but
I'm totally deranged.

I see the fires burning
I'm learning to love
but I can't stop this hate
coursing through my brain.

It's rough and twisted
it treats me like a bitch
but then I lick it
I say give it up
give it to me
give it over before
I have a fucking fit

and then my knees give out
and the floor breaks my fall
——ouch!

Bruised & Bloodied

jam my head thru a window, drive my fist thru a wall, i call you again & again & theres always nobody there
i paint the world red, i paint it black & green, running to the end of the line, cuz i need you here with me
im scared & alone, shivering & hollow, lost & on the run, thru skidrow & back, up & down the afterlives, all over the fuckin place, worried & sick
i know ive gotta stick w/ it, ive gotta fight even tho the odds are restricting me & holding me & keeping me shallow
i know she thinks of me, even tho the thoughts are probly laced w/ rage, i know she cares—cares not enuff to call. but she aint there, she aint here, & its scary & im free
Self-Destruct, Fuck Shit Up, Kill a Commie, Kill a Cop, Kill a man a woman a boy a girl, stomp em w/ my boot
stomp myself until im blue in the face, blue w/ rage a redness invading the dark, & there goes my head, crashing into that wall again
why do i do that? why do i let her absence get to me? shudnt it be a liberating thing, being free to be me, free to be somebody, free to walk away & not be a slave to her twat anymore?
shudnt it feel good, i mean shes gone & now youre here & theres not a thing you can do
i pogo at the shows
hang out w/ the boys
dance till we/re a fusion of sweat

Bruised & Bloodied

but for what>>>   it all seems so pointless futile worthless going nowhere & if she was in front of me, if she was here, there, now, somewhere, anywhere i cud see id reach out to her & wrap her up in my manly embrace & ... but shes not there shes not here, & its driving me fuckin madd
im off my rocker, off of my ass, im swinging & flailing, stomping & thrashing, & its so pointless i know I dont even see the point, so there goes my head, cocked back & swung forward crashing smashing bashing into that same fuckin wall again,
and......................................

A Plan for Greatness

I'm sinking—where's
my life vest when I need it.
Where's my anchor that will
keep me grounded but lost
at sea to the best of the freaks
I give credit to. I wonder
do you wonder?
what happened last year
last night
the world swirling and making me dizzy
it's such a fright.
I walk on the swirling river
as it winds a path around my head.
I follow the rapids as they take me
straight down to HELL>>>
I watch the world as it erupts in acid that
eats away at society's insides.
The river brings me through the madness
in solitude untouched by the bad bad world
that's around us. We walk together
only not forever, because we will separate when
it's time and when it's time
my mind will undulate and shudder
like a blunt instrument
coming down across my head.

A Plan for Greatness

So I say to you
with my last breath
what's the point of all the violence
all the strife
all the war....
Why go on living when
someone'll just strip away your right
to a happy and peaceful life?
Why do anything when a war
is roiling around the corner? just
waiting for you to step outside.

I walk on the water feeling like Jesus Christ
I sometimes wish I could die for your sins
just at the chance of being a lasting memory
at a chance at being someone more than
me
me
and I got it I really do. I got a plan
to make me the man to be
remembered....

Why is there so much hatred going
on in this sacred sphere?
Why are people waging war
when we could gather around
and have a beer.
Why not just take a gun and stick
it in your fucking mouth
pull the trigger and say
goodbye world I've just had enough.
Or spray a volley of bullets into your school
and take down your oh so innocent peers
who were not so innocent when they kicked your down
and strung you up in a locker until

Jeremy Void

someone found you there.
Then when all is done, you bite the bullet
as it splices through the back of your head
——there's no turning back anymore....

When I feel like God I have these dreams
more like schemes
more like nightmarish realities
that will turn the world on its head
and I could die be dead
and be a memory ...

but it's beyond me
gone way over my head....

The Holy Ghost

Don't you laugh at me....
There's a method to my madness
a course for my action///

where you see sadness I see
growth/
where you see trouble I see
strength/
where you see insanity I see
brilliance/ I see a new way of being

I see the waning light in the madman's eyes
I see the declining heart that throbs
      deep inside the slut's chest>>>>
      behind years of neglect and abuse

I see the dried-up tears dripping beneath
the psychopath's eyes
I listen to the sun, it speaks to me....
it tells me things you would never dreams of
things you could never come to terms with
      you will die not knowing
      die ignorant and blissful
      deceased and in the heaven of the gods

Jeremy Void

as I watch the pirate ship sink and the men
on board die in the assaulting abyss

they cry and scream and fight to stay afloat
as I shed one yearning tear at the hope that
they make it to the next….
        that they carry on like bandits
        and thieves
        and bad men in the eyes of the noble

but I see a light, an evolving star, that looms
in the midst of evil, showering its iridescent glory
on the ones who choose a life of sin….

They are golden
they are great
they are the best
they are the chosen few….

They die for your sins >>>>>

A Song of Dreams

I'm all wound up
in tears.
The music's slow
droning and cold—
I feel sick
to boot.
Last night I
slept a full 22 hours
and my body feels
stiff
and my mind is
blank bleak unfolding
like a river—the future's
unwinding and I
deliver blow upon blow
so that it
doesn't find me but
I know it will but
I know it's behind me
but but but—but
I'm plummeting fast
fast
shattering myself around
this soundless future
this boundless destiny.

Jeremy Void

You can have
what's left of me
cuz I'm too busy
treading in yesterday's
world
tomorrow passing me in
a blur it's so sad.

I sit here and mope
remembering the rumble
as I croak and
fall apart.
I try to do the
right thing all the time
but I always fall
way too far left
every single time....................

I think living's just
a dream
and life is just
one scheme after another
and that other dream
       you know the one
that happened just the other day
       not yesterday but
      the day before
         I think, anyway
it seems much more interesting
      not here
      but there
I lived here way too long
long enough to sing this
same sad song
      a song of dreams.

A Song of Dreams

Yesterday
I was bad
life was rad
and I had just about
everything I could ever
want.
                        Whereas today
                        I'm lost
                        in a ong long track
                        of suffering.
                        I've treaded these tracks
                                trust me I have
                        for way too long
                        all the way down
                        my veins
                        my arms
                        and what's there is
                        too much pain
                              for me
                              to bear.

So I'm here
not there
keep it in mind that
what's here is just fine
my life as I know it, and
what's there might seem
more appealing
but only cuz I'm scared
of what tomorrow holds.

I will go forward you know
but only on a dare
but only if you would share
some of your hope

Jeremy Void

so that
it won't seem so terrifying anymore

but just don't let me go....

The Next Big Punk Rock Hit

Everything I do I do to destroy.
Everything I say I say to annoy.
It's all fun and games, if you ask me
IF YOU ASK ME. The end is coming and there's
nothing we can do to stop it.

So let's party with our cocks out.
Drink till we're vomiting blood.
Rip off our suits of nothing
Spit and rant and rave till we just drop dead
on the fuckin floor.

The president worships Satan
The senator is a Nazi
The police are beating up black men
And our teachers belong to the KKK

Nothing is relevant anymore
It's all just rhetorical nonsense
Needles and pills are all we live for
So let's take something that makes us kill

Let's all party with our cocks out.
Drink till we're vomiting blood.
Rip off our suits of nothing

Jeremy Void

Spit and rant and rave till we just drop dead on the fuckin floor.

<u>I can't stand your face.</u>

Junky Pride

I'm an escape artist
guess you could say
always escaping the present with
the drugs that I take
        always
              on the run from
reality the real world everything
you've come to know and love.

It's sad I know
sad so to resent living so
damned much.

I'm scared I'm scared.
The world spins with
      or without
         me existing .... it goes on
on and on and on, and I
just can't take it anymore
    so I run and I make
quite the living doing so.

Marketing the nightmare
and others   they laugh at
what I've been through

Jeremy Void

the fetes that I've crossed.
They laugh like it's all
just a joke   and it is
          just a joke
a silly thing that I've created.

A creation that costs
the world to uphold.
A project that consists of
endless projections that make
me sick to no end.

I run with the best
sink with the worst.
Drowning in oblivion as
I steal second base out
from under you, my friend.

We frolic in shit and
we live sickly falling apart
falling to death.... A sick sin that

it is....

We laugh in miserable droves.

I Am a Fish

I am a fish.
I thread my way around
the fish bowl.
People stare at me
from the outer world,
but I don't care because
I've got all I need down here.

I am a fish. A tiny black fish.
My world centered in this bowl.
I know nothing else, and yes
it's quite the sheltered existence,
but you know what, everything's already
taken care of for me down here.

Sometimes when the time is right
I mosey up to the walls and peer
out at the large-eyed creatures
staring in. They look weird to me.
They look strange and intriguing.
Every now and then I ponder
what it would be like to be one of them.
But then again, I am only a fish.

A tiny black fish.

For the Painter

I am a writer—
words are my craft
I use them to deploy images
to depict vivid landscapes
action from all sides.
I swing back the whip
and it lashes the page
painting words on the lines
scrawling image for image

> although sometimes I feel envious
> of the painter
> for the ability to capture a moment
> in time, with a few strokes of
> the paintbrush...

I am a writer, yes, but
as a writer I can only display
movement that runs laps
around your head.
I can display action, sure, but just
for once I would like to capture
a single moment in time.

Into the Madness

another night
another dream
another fright
ANOTHER scream

I delve into the madness,
thumbing through it as I pick which
deranged emotion I would feel
today———the morning is immense
the daylight breaching the sky
and I crawl back into my pillow
hoping for relief.

The day begins with a start.
I feel shaken and distraught, already
dreaming up a diabolical scheme to
partake in this evening.
Maybe spraypaint my name across
the sun and watch my fellow man
perish as it disintegrates.

The morning sometimes
makes me feel alive.
But mostly I feel deader than dead
——so dead

Jeremy Void

I feel kinda high and you know,
I never wanna die although I know
the inevitable is only
seconds away. Its ticking & ticking
as it gains momentum and will soon wash over me.

For Medicinal Purposes

1.
Why laugh when you can cry?
Why live when you can die?
I get tossed around from woman to woman.
Don't they know their whole existence
        is a lie....

2.
Spiraling down
I'm tumbling and I'm scared
Plummeting into
damnation, I burrow into
my own skin and hide.

3.
It's all just perspective
if you ask me.
It's all just inflexion
if you ask me.
It's just a case of
introspection, but

Jeremy Void

    don't you dare
    ask me because I'm
        sure to steer you wrong....

4.
Writing equals survival.
Reading equals satisfaction.
I'm heading down an
intellectual spiral that's taking
me farther into my own head
farther into my own skull—
the walls are breaking down
the walls are letting me in and I see
I see the things
that make
me tick
        and I don't like it
        so I think I'll go back to bed.

Not Good Enough

If I was only a foot taller, maybe an inch thinner, a bit better looking, or had a larger dick, I might feel a little bit better about being me, about being here, and living now, but truthfully I dream about being him, being there, and living then.
If only I was smarter, had a car, and some cash that could buy me that, then I might feel more alive, feel higher, and farther, and I might want to be in these shoes, but these shoes never seem good enough.
More hair, more muscles, more drugs, more drugs, more drugs, so I could be someone else and someone else and someone else, but that guy he's got one less leg and one less eye, and that woman is missing a tit and she's living in a shack that I'd rather not have.

If only a bomb fell I might feel better about this hell, but the bomb wasn't wide enough and didn't carry a big enough blast and now only half this country has been destroyed and it's just not good enough.

My Psychedelic Suicide
inspired mostly by music created by and artwork handpicked by my good friend Ben Gustafson

1.
the demonic sembiotic spine
threaded thru your mind,
twisting & retching as it
reaches into the sky
has got me lost in a whirlwind of lies
poking thru my eye
making me cry unfortunate tears
that wisp down my back
treading electric webbing
kinetic & spherical
a swirling of emotions going
up into me like spicy blades
of sonic might. of ultra disarray that
wraps its ultra-sonic rays all the way around
my head. blistering & vicious
it hits me w/ a kick strong enough
to lift the plates that carry the earth
in a sort of cocoon—a blue & green ball
that bounces as if made
of rubbery film, bubbling over
explosive to the point of imploding.
im lucid & destructive

My Psychedelic Suicide

a mix of black & white force
that bleeds gray all over the city streets.
im lost in an ambient spin
lost in a patriotic backfire
the shit is coming back up &
spilling all over the central nervous system.

2.
the owl sits up on its perch
watching me thru foggy eyes.
the hawk dies & flops on the ground
as bats frolic amid the death & the
owl hoots & sneers in mock unisons to
the mayhem.   a fox pokes its head out
of the whales stomach, w/ a foamy grimace.
its sick so sick.
its sad so sad.
the whale mutates & grows
to the weight of the woocs
around it, bright & big
epically sieging & destructively
sound as everything breaks down
around it

i was walking thru the forest
listening to the sounds
the branches crunching
the leaves rustling beneath
my feet—stomp stomp stomp
clomp, goes the eagle searching
the wind blows & barrels
the egg hatches & out
comes a pterodactyl cawing & flapping

Jeremy Void

it wraps its wings around the earth
pulling it in & off it surges from
its perch in the leaves
CAAAAAAW.

hell rises.
the sky falls
crashing—smashing—
fanning out as the animals live
livid & sinfully devoted
to destruction.

i listen, standing on
the edge, at the beginning, in
the cave i stand on the epoch
awaiting change, & something breaks
CAAAAAAW, says the pterodactyl, a devil
lish beast reaching its wings &
casting a diabolical scheme of maddening
breaches, the world is beached

BEACHED
BEACHED
BEACHED
BEACHED

i shut down
my mind falls apart
i sit up
my head drops & hits
the concrete w/ a plop
the beast is in
the beast wins my right
& i wonder why

My Psychedelic Suicide

i let it....

the heavens come to life
the angels flap & strive
the world beneath it
swirls deeply in the sacrileg ous
manner it is known to roll
w/.

the riot begins here.
the angels come down.
the hawk is riveting & bright
the bats are free for strife.
your world melts
whereas mine grows stronger & harder
sound enough to withstand your
wrathful ways—hahahahahahaha

i live in the sky
i live in the mind
the whys have told me lies
& i wonder what brought me
here
this
madness

surfs up dude.

the waves roll past hell while
the demons laugh so hard
they fall harder & the angels
are up there shooting arrows from
their flaming bows which morph into
snakes that take a bite out of crime.

Jeremy Void

i live in the sky.
your mind is mine.
i wonder why this is life
but it is
it is
it is

because i said so.

the fire ignites
pacifies
the oceans are a bright blue
as the boats slue on the surface
of the abyss like eels
rolling   like snakes & boots
coming down & crashing into my my my
fuckin suicide.

3.
the sky breathes
harsh hypnotic breaths
seeping out of the systematic
tornado. the air gets tighter
wrapping me in its tendrils
dripping w/ sweaty morphine
i sit in the clouds running for
my deadly sins speeding up
riotous & curingly thunderously
apeshit raisins.

i sit in the sky, rain falling around me
i sit in the clouds, thunder & lightning
ricocheting off the blue beyond

My Psychedelic Suicide

& i am in space

i go to sleep
but the sound of riotous tears hits & i awake
im sitting on my face
as my nose bleeds, succumbing to fear
my ears throb succumbing to soundless
might & riotous cucumbers
they wrap their plummeting ancestors
around me & lift me until
im plunging into the sky
rising to the ground, the world
rammingly vivid in its visceral sense.
my whole life i waited for this
the money comes to me when
i go to sleep at night. the world feels like
a bee sting when i live to
slooooooooooow for the apeshit reality you will
find me in when i run w/
motorcycles cutting a path thru the ice
rink.

the edge of the madness
pulsates in beauty, so horrifying
& delightful i rip out my eyes.
the sound is like an eardrum
bashes w/ bolts of toothpaste
stinging me & sending me
into planet neutron.

the air rattles & shakes
me, whipping me & breaking me
to the point of imploding & i sit in
the impotent beetle as pliers press
me trying to pull me out….

Jeremy Void

they can try.

but the beetle skitters on the
hardwood floor amid strikes
& flashes of thunder, amid
the pounding of lightnings biting
pressure as it roils & claws
& tinfoil surrounds you hardly
ever able to rip apart but i try....

& i try.

i try to match the mighty pull
i try to match the mighty rolling
of two tons of force coming down
on me harder than hard, than you
as your fat explodes & blubber plows me from
every direction, sent & disordered
mowing me down....

ill mow you down
ill mow you down
ill mow into you plowing
& disastrously destructive......

gonna zap you, dude///

gonna wrap you
like eminem wraps peanut butter
w/ bread.
the music is hard & i wonder
why it barks so crowded w/ feces
... loudly & hardly are one & the same.
the soundlesness crowds me on the subway
when i stand tall in the clouds

My Psychedelic Suicide

& watch as the whole earth
melts into jelly.
the jelly undulate beneath god's foot

his spikey toenails.

4.
silence—it roars
bright & loud & vicious
it soars—thru clouds
& over seas & down
in the valley it billows
& blunders, the thunder's thrashing
the lights are flashing, strikes of
lightning—& the sounds fade
dissipate blank & jaded.
the world—going retro
people infest it like children in
a playground running & fighting
biting its a rumble.
the silence the wonder the world
it goes underground drops off
as a new sound rises a pounding
a rasping
fierce & electronic
it feasts eating things that
fall away & fade into
oblivion—
the lights go out
the silence rumbles up
& out surfaces as the ground
undulates in epileptic strokes.
i speak i spoke—the people

Jeremy Void

are stoked they crawl & croak
reaching & retching arms spreading
rapidly wondering—thundering.
the silence speaks
feeds
wrecks havoc on the seers
the believers.
twisted churning & burning me up
into oblivion...

5.
the city sleeps...
i walk the streets alone,
feeling grim & bold
feeling alive & whole
feeling like a demon & the whole
entire world
belongs to me.

the moon paves a translucent path
straight thru the clouds,
a spotlight in the night, bright w/
terror & glee it makes me shiver
quiver
a sliver & a dip & a drop
i feel so bad....
bad to my liver
& im getting bigger.

i creep around the corner & the slight
cool makes me feel hot
makes me feel fearless & ready for
adventure—me & my music rising up

My Psychedelic Suicide

& immersing me w/ fast, melodic sounds.

its an ugly night,
& i love it.
its a frightful sight
but it brings me cheers
& that i cant let down

not now
not then
not yesterday or tomorrow
cuz the now is delightfully sound
wrapping me up in barbed wires
lifting me off my feet & spinning me around
around
around.

i feel for the night
& it feels for me.
i feel it pulsating in my veins
we are one & the same.

the night & i are out tonight
& we wont be stopped
bargained w/
or bought
cuz theres only one thing
that we want————

a nightly adventure
w/ a nightly tune to overlay it
& then ill go home

& ill never sleep again.

Jeremy Void

6.
immersed in flies
the music like a shrine
a distraction from the invasion of flies.
i sit in the ill apartment, in the
hustle the bustle the flux of filth arising
& i think im dying....
the world like wax, the sun like
flames of volley & its coming
down on me fast.
the music fading & my mind, ablaze
with disharmony, fazes in & out
in & out, too quick like a siege of
waves roiling in the sea, gaining size
strengthening & brightening &
———disintegrating like the devils nectar//
distraught, in a world not of my own
in another world a world big & fat
growing out of proportion as it kicks your ass.
the flies crawl on the waste
crowding the garbage like vermin.
its sick & makes me sick.
i needa fog the place, a billowing, gray smoke
growing out of the nozzle.
toxic & killer, it kills & destroys the flies.
i sit in the midst of the buzzing swarm.
the flies clinging to discarded soda cans.
empty coffee mugs im in such a jam.
the trash is overflowing.
the ground is covered w/ paper & trash.
cleanliness cant be found here as
i huddle in this wasted life dissipating
fazing in & out & in & out, & spiraling
spiraling
spiraling

My Psychedelic Suicide

spiraling around my head im dizzy from the sickening
mess that covers every square inch—cant get
the dishes because if I try
the flies billow up & swarm me
get in my nose
my mouth
my ears its so freaking gross.

what am i to do?

7.
in a labyrinth the size of my head
the doctors search for meaning
they search for purpose
they search for reason, but they cant find their way
out——
its just too complex.

in a labyrinth the size of my head
many good men get lost, men w/
high degrees following the paths that my brain
shapes & forms & spins around
& around
& around, but they cant find their way
out——
its just too complex.

in a labyrinth the size of my head
thoughts mow thru the lanes like ghosts
evading the doctors, the psychiatrists,
cuz you cant psycho-analyze me
you cant put me under the microscope
cuz the things that make me tick are

Jeremy Void

the things that make me tick & in this maze
youll find that they arent very sane....
they bite & they stab & they sting.
the doctors curse.
the doctors search
& search
& search, but they cant find their way
out——
its just too complex.

ive devised a labyrinth, spun a web
of thoughts, so devious & perverse, something
for the doctors to converse about, something
for them to say about me.
something something something
something, but i cant find my way
out——
its just too complex.

8.
solitude—4 walls.
plain.
insane.
lacking anything
to which i can relate....
the padded walls of a dream
i bounce from wall to wall
my straightjacket tight &
holding me in

i sit on the edge of madness
          on the epoch of
             paranoia—these voices

My Psychedelic Suicide

following me down the road.
i hear things—& this
makes me crazy?—im really jus
lazy
my life in a haze. i bathe in
blood dont make me mad
jus sad
so sad....
sad sad sad
im bad   really really bad.

sounds—coming at me
from all sides they bite
they rip
they nip at my skin—yip yip yip......................

im running
times running out
the clouds overhead
smother me lock me in———im
stuck treading guts of a dream....
its only a dream i say.
its jus a dream i repeat.
i shout i scream, i stomp my feet
on the bone layered floor.
the dungeons holding me in
the doors jammed & i slam
bam bam thank you maam
i ram into them they creak.
the floor morphs & im floating
the river flowing beneath me.
i walk on water
or air
the whirlwind is swirling
& lifting me up—& I go up up up

Jeremy Void

flipping flying crying
the whole world explodes
i feel low
the bombs blow holes
in my head my mind.

im wasted now
dilapidated
so goddamn agitated.

its only a dream i say.
its jus a dream i repeat.

they lock me in a hole
away from reality, & i
beat the bars bang the bars
thwack them hard.
my knuckles char
break apart
i sit on the dungeons floor
weeping
peeing
& then i bend
& spew——& i know im
      done for....

9.
i wake up.
i sit up.
my head aches.
my body melts.
my mind dissipates
as the brain undulates

My Psychedelic Suicide

& my legs break crack crunch
& bunch together & i trip & go down
straight down——ouch.

10.
in a trance—
i see stars....
i see the sun
i see you & what you are
& i cant stand for it
anymore,
so i kick over tables & chairs
i have a fit, i throw a brick
i break the television set—who needs it
anyway.

in a trance—
i see the world for what it is
for the first time ever.
for the first time ever i rise above it
above the madness that ricochets off walls
& the floor double-crossed & i stop stop stop
stop it but it comes back up & spins around me
the spin quick & limber whipping me off my feet
& i flop—drop—clomp—plop—it hits me hard
on the head....
you think id be dead.
youd think so but
im coming back forya....

Jeremy Void

11.
the world unfolds around me
the worlds mold into something more
it snaps & whips & quick-steps me
all the way to babylon & im alive
the pimps & whores pass me by
& im alive
i ride my skateboard thru babylon city.
everyone stares at me like
im some kinda freak.
like im the freak?
this is babylon, home of the freaks
cretins
& creeps crawling up the walls as they conspire
to pounce....
& im the freak?
look at me riding my skateboard
thru downtown hell, fires rippling past me
high tides trilling up & up & up
up up up—higher than the sky.
im alive, an eyeball follows me as i ride the board
it watches me as i flee
up the street.

crowds suddenly coming at me like a wall
i hit them head on & take a sudden
dive into the bustle the riffraff stirring a storm
of a thing as i go splat on the moon.
soon i will understand but for now
its lost on me & im lost in space.
this gleeful bee has got me pinned to
the ground, it laughs & mocks & jokes
& hawks a ludicrous loogy in my face.
the wad of grossness splatters in my eye
i try to push myself up but the laughing bee

My Psychedelic Suicide

is too strong & holds me there as more bees
flock the happy one & say let go of em mannnn.
let go of em, leave em be—no pun intended says
one hairy one as it rises & fires a dart that
clips the gleeful one
& pins him to a tree——& im up
& running, running for the hills, the hills growing
as i come closer & closer, the sandy plains
wobbling beneath my quick-moving feet, hitching
kicking
pushing & jabbing
ramming one foot after another, &
im swept up by a crazy blast of wind pulling me
up & releasing me as i sail the skies my shirt
fanning out to create a cape as i soar the seven
skies the sun bright & warm & it winks at me.
the bees are on my tail & another crazy blast
of wind pushes into me & i wobble wobble wobble
my shirt rips & im falling, flailing, plunging to
————————to my horrible
ridiculous
somewhat ironic
demise that w/ a jolting pressure surges up &
meets me halfway there—the ground breaks
my fall, my collision breaks my legs, & my face plunges
into the pavement & cracks three teeth.
i smile all toothless but it was worth it—
thats Xtreme sports forya, getting on a skateboard
in the first place signs off on the risks of
a devastating face plant that leaves me a broken
mess.

i get up & brush myself off
jus to see that Babylon hasnt changed
one bit since i was gone.

Jeremy Void

12
.immersed in darkness
i sit in the pub & listen
to the country tunes
bleating outward & trilling
as the two men onstage
sing harmoniously.
            i wait in the dark
            my time
            my day
            has yet to start.

the sharp guitar riff
cutting thru ice
& knocking down glaciers im awake
      i think
im asleep—more likely the case.
a hailstorm of progressive
notes and cords coming to life
slithering deep in the backroom
a quivering shiver trilling
quietly up my spine frightfully
designed to demolish buildings
like a j-j——j-j——j-j-j-jackhammer
ramming thru steel & concrete
arriving on the other side
of mayhem deep its delicious
      & delightful
a bite a stab a tear a break in the
   fabric wound tight
   around me—gonna create
   chaos as the song pumps
& jabs into me it stings
deeply
sensationally

My Psychedelic Suicide

delighted to know you

i wonder in the dark
as the relentless jam slam dunks
a ricocheting funklike tumor springing up
from deep in the sea i wonder—
the song stops & ceases

and thank god for that……………………………………………………………..

To Be a Household Name

I wanna be featured
in a compilation
the name **Jeremy Void**
appearing in a book
    I myself
        did not produce.

Open it up and see my name
in bold above a list:
    Jeremy Void
      "A Dreamer, a Schemer, and a Freak
      "An Imperfect Circle"
      "Junky Pride"
      "Words That Heal"
        etc.   etc.

2015, does such a thing
even exists today?
Do people still even make
those kinds of things?
    still even care
      about poets
        in this day & age?

I wanna be featured

To Be a Household Name

in a book not of my own making.
    I want people to
    open it up, get intrgued
    by the name **Jeremy Void**,
    read my work, and then
        go online and
        buy my books.

I wanna be famous someday
I want a cameo on TV shows like
    Family Guy
    The Simpson
    a joke at my expense.

Wouldn't that be sick
if I got to appear on a talk show?
Got to speak my mind on
shows like Jay Leano
Got the chance to tell
the world what I thought....

People my whole life have
told me I should have my own
talk show,,,,   like Garrison Keillor
    maybe

told me I should be
a comedian cuz some of the things
I say are downright funny....

I want you to know who I am
    is all
I strive to be
a household name
    someday.

Jeremy Void

I want my name to
ring a bell to you
have an association
>	so that when you hear it
>	you think of certain things and say
>	to yourself where have I
>	heard that name before.

<u>But not at the expense of
selling out</u>....

www.ingramcontent.com/pod-product-compliance
Lightning Source LLC
Chambersburg PA
CBHW051753040426
42446CB00007B/346